KW

GARDENS IN AUSTRALIA

DEN S

TRALIA

SARAH GUEST PHOTOGRAPHY BY SIMON GRIFFITHS

For Richard James Chester Guest
1962–1983

First published in Australia in 2001 by
New Holland Publishers (Australia) Pty Ltd
Sydney • Auckland • London • Cape Town
14 Aquatic Drive, Frenchs Forest, NSW 2086
   Australia
218 Lake Road. Northcote, Auckland
   New Zealand
86 Edgware Road, London W2 2EA
   United Kingdom
80 McKenzie Street, Cape Town 8001
   South Africa

National Library of Australia
Cataloguing-in-Publication Data:

Guest, Sarah L. (Sarah Louise).
Gardens In Australia

Includes index
ISBN 1 86436 578 1.

1. Landscape gardening – Australia.
2. Gardens, Australian.
3. Gardens – Australia – Design. I. Griffiths,
   Simon (Simon John). II. Title.

712.60994

Publishing Manager: Anouska Good
Commissioned by: Derelie Evely
Project Editor: Jennifer Lane
Designer: Guy Mirabella
Production Manager: Janelle Treloar
Reproduction: Pica Digital, Singapore
Printer: Imago, Singapore
Set in Granjon and Didot

ACKNOWLEDGEMENTS
With thanks to Jo Baillieu, Primmy Bright,
Burke's Backyard, Derelie Evely, Anouska
Good, Jennifer Lane, Michael McCoy,
Guy Mirabella, Lady Potter, Gillian Russell,
Leo Schofield, Andrew Seccull, Caroline
Simpson OAM, Noela Sheperd, The Hon.
Rose Talbot, Dr Peter Valder, Wayne Walters
of the Ballarat Botanical Gardens in Victoria,
Miguel Garcia and Anna Hallet of the
Royal Botanic Gardens Sydney library
and many others including the garden
owners and designers who have given
so freely of their time and expertise.

Cover image: the coastal garden of Fiona
Brockhoff and David Swann. Image pages
2 and 3: Wigandia, the garden of William
Martin. Image pages 4 and 5: *Eucalyptus
leucoxylon* in the garden of Diana and
Michael Lempriere. Image this page: a view
through the garden of Diana and Michael
Lempriere. Image page 8: detail of a dry-stone
wall in the coastal garden of Fiona Brockhoff
and David Swann. Image page 11: a planting
of low-growing succulents in the garden of
Janice Morrison.

CONTENTS

THIS BOOK does not presume to mark some moment in time, to record or analyse the

history of garden styles, or to find the definitive trend for Australian gardens of the 21st

century. Indeed if, in any small way, it does any of these things, its authors, Sarah Guest

and Simon Griffiths, will be both surprised and gratified. The book came into being

because both creators and publishers thought

the project a worthy and fascinating one. All

INTRODUCTION

stood in awe of the courage, acquired skills,

creative talent and plant knowledge of

Australian gardeners, and wished to record the huge variety of gardening endeavour to

be found under the one heading of *Gardens in Australia*. Australians have been making

gardens on their huge and ancient continent for over 200 years. And making them in

almost every imaginable situation, climate and soil type. During this period, these

gardens have developed from the early, practical gardens of survival and protection

to the extensive ornamental 'useless' gardens of the modern merchant prince.

No one style has dominated—no one climate or condition prevails. Many different cultures and times have influenced the creative process. Fashions have come and gone as they do everywhere, at all times. Plant palettes have ranged from a world base to the restricted pickings of a particular locality, and continue to do so.

Perhaps more than most, Australians are aware that gardens are often temporary triumphs. In Australia, the extreme forces of nature are always there in one form or another. Some can be anticipated and controlled, others cannot—and they can spell the instant end to a life's work. Flood, drought, fire, storm, sand, salinity, disease and chronic erosion all wait in the wings. Always.

Moreover, the economic history of particular regions and the continent as a whole has been variable, to say the least. Gold, wool, mining, tourism and merchant know-how have each brought their respective prosperities and, in their wake, great and glorious gardens. But the downturns, depressions, recessions and 'corrections' have been just as pronounced and, in garden terms, have often proved devastating. Moreover, it is a mobile society, and few can hope to live in the one place for a lifetime.

Nevertheless, in the face of these challenges and conditions, Australians have made and continue to make gardens. Great gardens. And as this book shows, their designs and plants are as different as the conditions under which they live.

While the gardens are markedly different in appearance, two things unite their creative owners. The first relates to their attitude towards the environment. Though the practical implications differ from one person to the next, without exception, those interviewed during the course of this book's creation spoke of a desire to preserve and protect the native flora and enhance the habitats of native fauna. Their gardens might be composed almost entirely of exotic plants, but all were aware of what could damage the local environment—now or in the future. All recognised the burden of responsibility and all worked within some recognised parameter. The second unifying factor relates to climate. All worked within their particular climate and conditions—some of which were extraordinarily challenging.

The results speak for themselves, and it is our hope that this book will adequately recompense these skilled, knowledgeable and creative enthusiasts for finding time to share their talent with others. And, at the same time, illustrate the amazing variety of styles, plants and situations that influence the creative gardeners of Australia.

Sarah Guest and Simon Griffiths

THE TOPOGRAPHY OF Victoria's Western District varies between the bleak, the

boring and the beautiful; the mighty and the magnificent; the rolling and flat; the treed

and treeless. The landscape has huge scale and majestic presence. The climate is tough,

with fairly constant strong winds, cold winters, hot summers and the occasional all-

stunting drought. Banongil Station sits in the heart of this strong, demanding landscape.

It was—and remains—one of the Western District's great wool-producing properties.

But, at the home station on the banks of Mt Emu Creek, the land takes on an unexpected

and delicate prettiness. Steep creek banks are edged with weeping willows (*Salix*

babylonica), ancient river red gums (*Eucalyptus camaldulensis*) and great clumps of

daffodils. The scale is small and cosy and there is a beguiling sense of sheltered delicacy.

Vast skies are reflected in small pools. It is very painterly, and in spring, when the willows

sport emerald-green streamers, the prunus veils of pale blossom and daffodils dance,

it becomes a place of enveloping enchantment. Platypus play in the creek. Frogs croak and plop into water. Brolgas pose in nearby paddocks. Chestnut-breasted shelduck, looking too bright and too enamelled for reality, stand watchfully still. Magpies carol, kookaburras caterwaul, wattlebirds caw, cockatoos chat lazily, lorikeets screech through the sky and topsy-turvy blue wrens flit about near the shadows. And when black swans strut about on the lawn, the place looks like a Rupert Bunny painting.

But even at the height of spring, this garden's charm is never over-creamy. The gutsy design, grand scale, extensive use of bluestone and brick-red scoria, mature trees including huge palms, dense plant arrangements, disciplined lack of any extraneous statuary and the grand view to the paddocks combine to prevent even a hint of curdling charm. Moreover, the solid shelter-belts of flowering gums (*Eucalyptus leucoxylon*) add a shadowy sense of mystery to this unusual, strangely mystical, site. And, fortuitously, their dusty-red flowers pick up on shades used within the garden.

In about 1906, when Australia rode on the sheep's back, Charles Fairbairn, a member of a well-known pastoral family, greatly extended the homestead from its origins as a tiny bluestone shepherd's hut and laid out the grand Edwardian garden. He planted palms and what Diana refers to as 'cabbagey things' on his impressive front lawn and edged one side of it with a massive bluestone pergola. His son C.O. Fairbairn inherited his enthusiasm, and with his English wife Irene developed a keen interest in daffodil breeding. (They are reputed to have paid £56 in prewar money for a single bulb!) It was they who, between the wars, added the remarkable terraced daffodil garden.

When Michael and Diana Lempriere took on the property in 1975, the garden was in decline, although many of the daffodils had

OPPOSITE TOP: Huge Canary Island date palms (*Phoenix canariensis*) give the garden a strong, gutsy, Edwardian character. In contrast to many grand gardens of this period, the broad horizon is used to enhance the garden's design. OPPOSITE BELOW: Daffodils envelope the summerhouse. ABOVE TOP: A path edged with massed plantings of *Helleborus orientalis*. ABOVE: Beneath the boughs of an Algerian oak (*Quercus canariensis*).

been planted out on the creek banks in the fifties and were thriving. For a time, while small children grew and the Lemprieres studied the grammar of garden design in Italy and England, the garden remained much as they had found it.

Today, however, things are very different. The garden has been re-created, and although it remains recognisably Edwardian in character, much has changed—and changed for the better, without the affectation of numerous era-appropriate artefacts.

The drive, which winds though native parkland as it approaches the home station, now terminates in an elegant sheltered courtyard and at what was once a back door. From the front of the house, there is an uninterrupted view to the paddocks that lie beyond the garden with its exotic trees and elegantly bridged creek. The huge lawn is still there and kept in stupendous condition. Although some of the original trees have gone, replacements have been planted and, aided by a new watering system, are growing well. The great pergola with its solid bluestone pillars met with an accident quite recently, and has had to be rebuilt. Some minor improvements were made to the original proportions—minor improvements that constitute a major improvement in the overall scale of the edifice.

The terraced daffodil beds, screened from the front garden by a huge evergreen escalonia hedge, have had their bluestone retaining walls repaired and are once again densely filled with narcissus. Iris and hyacinths have been added to defuse any hint of the 'egginess' that can arise when there is a super-abundance of daffodils. Clipped lavender and rosemary bushes have been added for their strong architectural form and durability during the summer months.

A dense hedge of berberis separates the rose garden from the daffodil beds. It is a clever choice—the berberis withstands the harsh conditions with grace, and its red–purple leaves look well with the red–purple new growth of the rose bushes. A row of handsome hornbeams has been planted to mark an important path. These are clipped and pruned with care and constancy, and at some future date will form high arches framing the view to roses and daffodils.

Perhaps the most fascinating addition from the garden enthusiast's point of view is a coiling path that lies like a hose or snake across the bottom edge of the great lawn, linking the two side paths so that the wanderer can walk with dry feet right around this major space.

OPPOSITE TOP, LEFT TO RIGHT: The flowering gums (*Eucalyptus leucoxylon*) of an old shelter-belt, provide much more than shelter; An olive (*Olea europaea*) inhabits a Mediterranean pot. OPPOSITE BELOW, LEFT TO RIGHT: Prunus petals and old rollers; An invitation written in brick, stone, iron and timber.

In design this path takes nothing from the gardens of England or Italy and everything from an Australian ethos. It looks right here—it is of its time—it suits. Few notice it and it goes unremarked precisely because it looks so comfortable in this garden and in this place. Like many of the other paths in the garden, it is covered with the local scoria and kept clean, well raked and well edged.

Happily, the grand old house has always sat well down into the ground, but today it enjoys an even more intimate relationship with the garden. On the east face, a brick paved terrace decorated with potted plants and a few well-controlled, well-chosen 'strays' form a strong link between the house and an open, spreading lawn. Magnificent mature Algerian oaks (*Quercus canariensis*) sit at either end of the grass, which is corralled with a hip-high bluestone wall under-planted with agapanthus. The area has been designed to provide an inviting link between the inside and outside—and it does.

The garden at Banongil, with its essentially Edwardian character, has benefited greatly from the attentions of a modern, educated, artist's eye. Nowadays it abounds with appropriate and elegant arrangements of plant colour and form. Even the old lawn-rollers loll in well-placed elegance.

Care is taken to link the colours of the landscape to the greens of the garden. Buddleja species with grey–green leaves, pride of Madeira (*Echium candicans*) and the Iowa crab (*Malus ioensis*) are all used extensively for this reason. Dense clumps of hellebores (*Helleborus orientalis* cultivars) are massed in broad flurries beside a path. And the path, which might otherwise look lost beneath its canopy of mature trees, acquires considerable stature with these decorative flowery ribbons. *Helleborus foetidus,* with its taller, more angular growth habit, deeply serrated leaves and luminous green flowers, is given a different placement. It makes its presence felt in mixed borders and in single, striking clumps. Pale, creamy narcissus are used in the beds close to the house. Further away, the brilliant yellows of daffodils and wattles make music together.

Summer brings stronger shapes, forms and shades—Diana describes it as 'the tough canna look'. The plants have to be tough and no-one minds if they look it. Succulents are used in impressive pots, each inhabiting a pot chosen to display its particular attributes. The shade of terracotta used on the house picks up on the dusty red shade found in the local scoria, the bricks of the old architecture and the flowering gums. And the colour, in various strengths, is picked up again in the gardeners' shed and summerhouse by the creek. The matt dark-green found in tough foliage and in a shiny form by the great escalonia hedge is employed again on much of the woodwork.

ABOVE: The Wisteria Walk and white arum lilies (*Zantedeschia aethiopica*) in mid spring.

As a result, the house sits into its magical site and garden with an easy grace rarely associated with red-brick Edwardian grandeur.

The placement of the small trees scattered on the lawn has nothing to do with the suburban treatment of 'specimen trees', and everything to do with scale, emphasis, history and planting for the future. (Many of the magnificent mature trees are approaching senescence. Some have already gone.) A single prunus carrying bright cerise-pink flowers has been added to the froth of pale blossom, adding focus and giving guts to the arrangement.

As it stands, the garden at Banongil provides a good example of what happens when people who fully understand the grammar of garden design know when and how to break or bend the rules. Today this garden is a wonderful exposition of scale and proportion, point and counterpoint, straight and curved lines, strong design and effective plantings, shade, shadow and brilliant light.

At least that is what the visitor sees. It is always different for the owner, and when I visited during Diana Lempriere's absence she left me the following note:

> … *a lot of big old trees have fallen and the stone pillars, hedge etc. came down recently. Rabbits have eaten creeper off the big garage. Possums devastate all the climbing roses. Suggest you return in 50 years for a good result.*

BELOW: The modern serpentine path that separates the great formal lawn from the more informal creek banks. In concept, the path's design is highly original but, being both appropriate for an Edwardian garden and well suited to the setting, it often passes unnoticed.

BALA

THE MOVE FROM INNER Sydney with its crowded spaces and heavy air to a

cliff-top, oceanside suburb is one of only a few kilometres. However, in terms of visual

surroundings, it is like moving to a distant, different, well-ventilated world. It's a move

Ann and Michael Duffett made some four years ago, choosing an exquisitely renovated

house set in suburban surroundings and exposed to all the ferocious salt winds the

nearby ocean can deliver. When the property was acquired, the garden consisted of little

more than the obligatory patch of grass at the front and a small, utilitarian yard space at

the back. The challenge was to create a front garden that would enhance the visually

impressive, colonnaded façade, while providing the occupants with some privacy and

visual protection from their suburban surroundings—not an easy task when the façade

might be thought best suited to a setting of rolling hectares. Moreover, when creating

gardens in the classical manner, it is easy to get the scale wrong and achieve a clumsy mismatch with the existing architecture, or to make the design so heavy as to look funereal, or so light as to lack a proper presence.

The same challenges existed for the area behind the house, but here there were the additional requirements of outdoor living space and a more attractive aspect for the pleasant everyday living room. Again there were problems. Space was limited and the outlook was dominated by a high boundary wall.

Clearly, in both areas, the design would have to be strong, and at the same time achieve some sort of harmony with the existing architecture. Scale and proportion would be of paramount importance. And a few visual tricks or diversions would be needed if these outside areas were to acquire enough stage presence to retain the eye and contribute some spirit of their own. The boring and useless had to go—a spirit of place was needed.

With these problems and aims in mind, a designer was selected. As the result of reading a press article on gardens designed by Paul Bangay of Melbourne and subsequently receiving his book *The Defined Garden* as a Christmas present from two young grandsons, Ann intuitively sensed that he was the right person for the job. Ultimately it was his design that not only fulfilled the demanding practical requirements but added a skilful touch that amounts to stage presence and correct character.

Today, as one approaches the house, little can be seen of the front garden. In fact the eye is led directly to the 'cour d'honneur' and the front door with its super-smart, paired, pot-grown bay trees. These formal, clear-cut, geometric shapes are slightly softened with the trailing evergreen stems of the white convolvulus (*Convolvulus sabatius* 'White Gladys') that flow over the sides of each pot and produce flower upon flower all through the warmer months. It is only when one turns away from the door and looks back that an eye-arresting garden designed in the classical manner is revealed—and it comes as a complete and enchanting surprise.

The grassed area has been exploited. A terrace now occupies the space and water, with its soft glitter and quiet music, modifies any perception of heat and glare.

(It's an old Arabian artifice, and here it is both necessary and successful.) A raised pond is surrounded by a thick band of orange jessamine (*Murraya paniculata*), clipped to the same height as the pond's flat stone lip. (Paul Bangay often uses plants to extend and add presence to architectural features. Here the orange jessamine hedge does all that—and does it in some style.)

A stilt hedge concocted from the Australian native tree *Ficus microcarpa* var. *hillii* screens the suburban street and draws the eye down towards the cool reflections on the space-enhancing water. The ground is covered with gravel and broken in the foreground with a chessboard pattern made from sandstone paving stones and another Australian native plant, *Pratia pedunculata*. (At least that is how it began. At present a clover-like weed is proving thriftier than the ground-hugging pratia.) Thick, squat, squared hedges of orange jessamine separate the gravel from the containing walls and give a tailored trim to the solid plantings of gardenias, azaleas and hydrangeas that shelter between the walls and these hedges. Swelling domes of box are used to emphasise, yet soften, important corners and angles.

This design—put into effect through the contrast between dark evergreen leaves and paler, man-made, stone-coloured shades—looks simple in the extreme, but is dependent on two of the most difficult things to get right: scale and proportion. The use of colour and seasonal flowers are of less importance in achieving this effect. There are flowers, of course, but with the exception of a red camellia (brought with affection from a previous garden and now adding a glow of warm colour in winter), these are all white. The style, like that of the house, is disciplined and strong, yet the delightful fountain figure obviates any suspicion of heaviness. The heady perfumes of gardenias and orange jessamines hang on the air and leave no doubt that this is indeed a place for plants.

Behind the house a classical, tailored look has again been adopted, with plants kept close to the walls to maximise space. It is hoped that a wisteria growing over a pergola and along the tops of the walls will ultimately provide shade in summer. Careful training will ensure that these plants look spectacular when in bloom and

BELOW: A pair of sweet bay trees (*Laurus nobilis*), clipped into stately lollipops, echo the existing scale and architecture of the 'cour d'honneur'.

that the leaves and stems add emphasis to the architecture at all times. Thus far, however, these plants are struggling in the savage salt winds that sweep across from the nearby cliffs. A Boston ivy (*Parthenocissus tricuspidata*) which half covers one wall is also feeling the draught.

Happily, Chinese star jasmines (*Trachelospermum jasminoides*) which are trained to form highly noticeable, boxed multiplication signs along the walls are thriving, and do much to give the back garden its lively, classical character. Huge pots stand on the pale stone paving and hold dark junipers (*Juniperus chinensis* 'Spartan'). A stone table—not the sort to be moved in a hurry—has a simple, white tiled surface with a discreet blue and yellow border. It is one of the few decorated surfaces in the entire garden, and these small blue flecks exactly pick up on the luminous blues of the sea skies that enhance the site.

This garden did not come into being by pressing an expensive, fashionable button, standing back and paying the bill. Neither Michael nor Ann had heard of Paul Bangay before they began their search for someone who could give their house an appropriate setting—a garden portraying modern classicism at its best and a place to enjoy as well as cherish. It was they who scoured shops and garden centres and, struggling to get the right scale, located the boy-statue. They were the ones who found the fourteen huge, matching pots that now give the design the important punctuation marks intended by Paul Bangay. (Take them away and the place would look bleak, bare and bereft—leave them in place and they hardly earn a second glance.) It was Michael and Ann who found the table—and the crane needed to put it in place! And they who instinctively knew Paul Bangay was the man for the job and who formed a working relationship with Peter Hatfield, who made it all happen.

Today the garden looks as if it had been designed with the house—or that maybe it was the other way round, and the house was designed to fit an existing garden! Either way, it is not a case of bringing the garden indoors or of taking the house outside. The two just fit together—an effect that depends largely on the achievement of perfect scale and proportion, together with the designer's ability to exploit the visual contrasts of different levels and incorporate the sight and sound of water.

BELOW: An Australian native, *Ficus microcarpa* var. *hillii*, is kept well clipped to form a compact screen between the front garden and the street.

MODE

RNIST

'AFTER A WHILE I feel like chopping them off—when the bay comes alive you

don't need them.' Fiona Brockhoff is speaking of the huge electric-blue flowers of

Echium candicans syn. *fastuosum* which, in her garden, without water or fertiliser, put on

a spectacular summer-heralding show. But flowers are not what this garden is about.

They are there—in plenty and in eye-catching glory—but they are incidentals. Part of

the place. When the coastal tea-tree (*Leptospermum laevigatum*) and the moonah

(*Melaleuca lanceolata*) bloom, this garden is embraced in a froth of white petals, but it

is their dark, irregular, twisting trunks, stripped of dead brushwood, that give the

place its distinctive spirit. Three varieties of *Aeonium arboreum*, with their generous

supply of great knobby yellow flowers, grow here. But no plant gains a place here because

it carries bright, abundant flowers over a long period. In fact such flowers may well face

an untimely chop. The garden is about space, sculpture and place—its own. Not flowers.

It sits high on a sand dune on Victoria's Mornington Peninsula.
Port Phillip Bay lies below—silver-grey in winter, a deep glinting
sapphire-blue in summer. On the other side, just one dune away, the
surf of Bass Strait reveals itself with a constant muffled thumping.
Above hangs a huge, ever-changing sea sky. A strong, clear light
pervades the open spaces. A shadowy, well-treed bush landscape,
where the indigenous slender greenhoods (*Pterostylis foliata*) carpet
the ground in spring, surrounds the garden.

The garden is also about using plants with a local genetic base and
experimenting with them. The coastal she-oak (*Allocasuarina
verticillata*), for example, may be used for topiary or the moonah may
be cut into balls or a clipped hedge.

Two major open areas are devoted to ornamental gardening and
act as 'buttresses' between the house and landscape. One, with a
northern and eastern aspect, is a self-contained terrace designed to
enhance the view to the bay. The other is embedded in and merges
with the surrounding tree-covered dunes. It takes the midday and
afternoon sun and lies on the ocean side of the house.

A terraced herb garden, which does double duty as a drying area, lies along one side of the house and links the two open decorated spaces. At a lower level lies a small vineyard, its square posts arranged like sculpture. Nestled into the trees is a raised kitchen garden with beds divided by massive old wooden piers. (In winter, when the veggies lie low, the place looks as if a giant's star-shaped brooch has fallen on the ground.) A small family of chickens have their domain close by—this garden is also about good food, healthy living and organic management.

And it is about working with the prevailing conditions (neutral limestone sands derived from the shells of billions of small marine creatures) and the existing climate: cool temperate, frost-free with winter rain, summer droughts and salt-laden winds that blow from every direction. It is about gardening with limited water, no chemical fertilisers and without human exhaustion. Today this theory is much talked about amongst gardeners but rarely put into practice. Here the mantra is followed and plants must be able to survive and thrive in these conditions to earn their place. As a result of this tough discipline, the garden, which is only four years old, looks mature and sits easily with the distinctive surrounding topography.

Such plants may be valued as single specimens or for what they can contribute to a group. Either way, all must add shape or texture

BELOW: Timber from an old pier, sand grit, moonah, cushion bush, *Correa alba*, *Stipa stipoides* and the local tea-tree (*Leptospermum laevigatum*) form a buttress between the 'garden' and the dunes. The blue flowers of the native hibiscus (*Alyogyne huegelii*) speak persistently of sea and sky.

to the composition. The fan-like rice paper plant (*Tetrapanax papyrifer*), the knobby club rush (*Isolepis nodosa*), the mat rush (*Lomandra longifolia*), cushioning convolvulus (*C. cneorum*), reedy dianellas, clumping correas, tufting poas and stipas and bulging succulents all find a place in the bright light. So does a spiky yucca. Once an ailing indoor plant, it has found new status and stature outside. Tree aeoniums with their huge rosettes of cabbage-like foliage grow to unusual sizes and weird shapes. Casuarinas cascade. Melaleucas and leptospermums brave the winds with an upward thrust.

The garden is also about working with recycled materials, local materials (there is no terracotta in this garden), found treasures and original works of art. And the many 'works of art' combine to make a single 'work of art'.

The whitish limestone walls used in both the garden and house make a strong link between the garden, house and surrounding landscape. Here the usual lines of demarcation between house, garden and surrounding landscape are blurred beyond recognition. It is the elements in common that are important.

Raked gravel grit from a local quarry is used on the flat surfaces and brings with it a beach-like atmosphere. The sand nearest to the dunes is flecked with tiny fragments of shell. Unloved decorative concrete pots created in the sixties were spotted, and their bemused owner persuaded to give them up. Here they gain importance and give the garden a slightly retro atmosphere. The spun copper birdbaths and planters designed by Fiona were brought into being by a craftsman whose previous forte was the production of lampshades for colonial theme parks! Copper is also used in the chains that serve as overflows to the water tanks, and the growing verdigris is valued for its sense of sea-exposed wear and tear. Limestone columns, the work of the renowned New Zealand sculptor Chris Booth, look like a natural part of this nature-embracing place.

Here utilitarian objects turn into sculpture too, and discarded objects become decorative. Massive wooden beams obtained when an old sea-soaked pier was demolished have become both a sculpture and a staircase. The finds of the beachcomber, sea-smoothed china and shoreline shells are gathered and grouped like a lyrebird's display. Odd bits of flotsam and jetsam, carefully but casually arranged, rot in the sun, with pride of place going to a Christmas tree made from washed-up thongs! (This was such a success with friends that the found thongs were supplemented with a few brand new bargains, leaving a very bewildered shop assistant who found it hard to understand that colour could be more important than size or having a matched pair!)

OPPOSITE ABOVE: *Zygophyllum billardieri* adds bright leaves and yellow flowers to the blue of the native hibiscus (*Alyogyne huegelii*). Cushion bush, *Stipa stipoides, Poa poiformis* and a mop-topped casuarina make a garden while the corrugated water tank with its verdigris overflow chain provides structure. OPPOSITE BELOW: Cushion thyme (*Thymus lanuginosus*) and old pier beams form muted stripes on 'red wash day'. *Santolina virens* adds humping bumps, bronze fennel adds a bit of fluff and an olive, artichokes (*Cynara scolymus*) and *Echium candicans* branch out.

Sturdy wooden sun lounges, usually such cumbersome and dominant articles, take on a casual lightness. One has been canvassed with green at the head end and blue at the base. On the other, its pair, the colour arrangement is reversed. The result is light, inviting, amusing. A drying red wash on the line looks as if it has come from an art gallery. Flicks of red coral lie on the sand grit and provide tiny focal flicks of colour. 'Those are my flowers,' Fiona says.

There are no contrived garden rooms here, no self-contained schemes, no sharp contrasts or visual arguments. It all fits. Moreover, there has been minimal damage, visual or organic, to the local environment. Nothing is over-the-top, extravagant or wasteful. The decorative elements are to do with shape, space, texture and sculpture. And it is these emphases, taking many forms and finding many manifestations, which prevent the garden from merging so completely with the bush as to pass unnoticed. Importantly, the garden demonstrates that dedicated environmentalists can create gardens that are beautiful, interesting and have an all-pervading sense of place. David Swann, Fiona's partner, is an engineer with a passion for the local limestone and recycled local materials. He does all the construction work which includes building the stone walls, making pavers out of shell-speckled sand grit and turning the timbers from old piers and jetties into retaining walls. And today the two of them are successfully employed designing and creating gardens that reflect their attitude to gardening and garden design.

Fiona retains few memories of her mother, who died while she was a small child. But she grew up in the garden her mother had created and feels that she inherited her mother's love of gardening, particularly her enthusiasm for echiums and spiky things. So in that sense the garden reflects the past; however, few design labels fit this garden, which is as much about philosophy as it is about decorative devices. But if modernist is defined as 'a tendency to subordinate tradition to harmony with modern thought', then this garden can proudly wear the label 'modernist'.

PREVIOUS PAGE: Fragments of coral lie like petals washed up on the shore. A New Zealand totem adds shape, height and scale to the richly textured scene. *Euphorbia characias* subsp. *wulfenii,* aeoniums and echiums grow to amazing sizes. *Senecio repens* and *Cotyledon orbiculata* flow over sand grit and between rocks. Echiums, the knobby club rush (*Isolepis nodosa*) and *Phormium* 'The Chief' point to the skies, while in the background *Lomandra longifolia* adds bulk and a pervasive perfume. Delicate looking, tough-as-old-boots, dusty miller (*Centaurea cineraria*) holds its own. OPPOSITE TOP, LEFT TO RIGHT: A granite bowl with *Correa alba*; Old fishing net floats with sea box (*Alyxia buxifolia*); The thong tree. MIDDLE, LEFT TO RIGHT: Chris Booth's limestone columns; Stone work; Round succulents in square pots. BOTTOM, LEFT TO RIGHT: Discards from the deep come to shore; A bottle collection; Jade plant (*Crassula ovata* 'Variegata') with pegs.

CONCE

AN OLD IRON BLUBBER BOILER of huge and bulbous proportions stands

beside the gate of an 1840s house in the suburbs of Launceston. (No-one worries

about theft—it took a crane and a burst water main to get the object into place.)

In many ways, this unusual but impressive ferrous artefact illustrates much of

the garden's character and much of this gardener's approach to making a garden.

Judy Humphrey's grandfather found this relic of the whaling industry on Bruny

Island many years ago. Somehow he got it back to Tasmania and presented it to

his wife. Then, long after her grandparents had left both their boiler and their

Hobart home, it was spotted outside the gate waiting for the waste collection. Once

again it was commandeered and given a new purpose in life. Today the boiler

functions as a self-contained pond, and throughout the summer months the scented

white flowers of water hawthorn (*Aponogeton distachyos*) dance on a dark surface.

Circular shapes are a recurrent theme here. They link spaces and levels and in the process, remind one of still ponds, expanding ripples, spreading lily pads, stepping stones and sunlit open spaces. Old round grinding stones become steps, small pyramids of round stones adorn quiet corners and circular brick 'platforms' provide cohesion and restful space. Even some of the plants seem to have a well-rounded presence. The exceptionally fine strain of *Euphorbia characias* subsp. *wulfenii*, which for all its seedy magnificence has produced only one seedling, is a case in point. The double hellebore known with affection as 'Betty R.' (for the great Tasmanian gardener, the late Mrs Edward Ranicar), also has a well-rounded presence. (It, in contrast to the euphorbia, seeds with energy and breeds true from seed nine times out of ten.)

Four years ago, when Judy left a cherished country garden and began remaking this one, a lawn lay below the large trees in front of the house. A *Magnolia grandiflora*, an ash and a liquidambar (a tree much chastised for its constant supply of spiky fruit-clusters) have remained—the lawn has not. Today large bricked circles lie on the ground, linked together by paths, stepping stones and steps, and surrounded by deep leaf litter and a wealth of select plants. Some circles are solid while some sport green hubs. One sports a hub of emerald velvet lawn chamomile (*Chamaemelum nobile* syn. *Anthemis nobilis*). All are decorative in their own right and contribute to an original design that provides a home for Judy's extensive collection of small plants. Moreover, the system allows all these precious plants to be seen without resorting to a fuss of fiddly paths.

This garden is full of textural interest and contrast. Stone, brick, rusting iron, gravel, wood and cane are used to great effect, as are plant containers made from hand-hewn stone and plant containers made by Judy that look like hand-hewn stone—both sorts grow moss. The bulbous sides of the great boiler are rusted, rough and light-absorbing, while the surface of the water within is smoother than stainless steel and softly reflective.

All articles are carefully sited and set off by dense groupings of carefully selected, often rare plants. The old boiler, for example, is surrounded by soft tufts of the unusual golden grass (*Hakonechloa macra* 'Aureola'), upright lemon-yellow ixias, tiny yellow pokers (*Kniphofia rooperi*) and striped grass (*Miscanthus sinensis* 'Zebrinus'). Above it hang the tiered branches of *Viburnum plicatum* 'Mariesii'. In this garden, there is always something to attract the eye and something to lead it forward. In this case, the single pale-yellow rose 'Fruhlingsgold' (which Judy describes as 'the best') leads the eye into the shady front garden.

In the once-concreted garden behind the house, many of the plants have to be container grown. Old laundry troughs, including one made from Huon pine, join the regular plant containers. A brake drum from an old steam engine (which leaks rather than drains) has become a small, self-contained bog garden filled with the black-stemmed *Alocasia amazonica* and the spear-like leaves of *Iris laevigata* 'Variegata', while an old hot-water cylinder encircles a yellow-flowered *Cantua buxifolia*.

Old weatherboard sheds shelter under a wealth of plants. *Forsythia suspensa* sprinkles the building with its stemless yellow stars in winter, while 'Cecily Lascelles', an Australian-bred Alister Clark rose with semi-single, warm-pink flowers, takes over in summer.

To the side of the house lie two small garden rooms, linked by steps. At the lower level, an old, now-nameless, pink camellia dictates the colour scheme. The statuesque *Melianthus major,* with its rust-red flowers, stands nearby, as does the equally statuesque *Geranium maderense*, with its dark, finely cut, fan-shaped leaves and firework-like display of cupped cerise flowers. Plants with dark leaves, including *Heuchera* 'Garnet' and *H.* 'Rachel', *Pelargonium* 'Samobor' with its dark brown leaf markings and *Eupatorium* 'Chocolate', are used to complement the hot-pink hues.

In the upper room, plants with yellow or white flowers set off a white marble statue. At ground level, the creamy-white wallflower (*Erysimum* 'Ivory White'), the white-flowered honesty and the form bearing white variegated leaves (*Lunaria annua* 'Alba' and *L.* 'Variegata') fluff about in spring. Wake robin (*Trillium grandiflorum*) and a white shooting star (*Dodecatheon meadia* 'Alba') stand elegantly erect, while *Corylopsis sinensis* var. *sinensis* 'Spring Purple' adds lemon flowers and rust-purple young leaves in spring. In summer the rose 'Graham Thomas' does its yellow-petalled thing with enthusiasm.

This garden is primarily about plants, but colour contrasts and colour companions, textures, tawny tarnishes and a far-from-it-all atmosphere also play a part. The white leaves of *Geum phaeum* 'Taft's Surprise', *Sisyrinchium* 'Aunt May' and variegated hostas and aquilegias with pale-golden leaves bring shafts of sunlight into the tree-shaded garden. And always shape is laid against shape, leaf against leaf and form on form. The effect is rich, subtle, musical, enduring. Flowers are always part of the tapestry in this garden; in fact, there is a bulb in flower every day of the year. Moreover, there is a gardener who knows what they are, where they are, how to make them thrive and how to integrate them into a bigger picture.

ADELAIDE IS AUSTRALIA'S rose-growing capital. The climate and slightly alkaline

soil appear to suit rose requirements, and in Adelaide roses seem to grow bigger, better,

healthier and be more floriferous than almost elsewhere else in the world. Even in the

strong light of this hot, dry climate the petals are as lush as any, and often the colours seem

slightly more intense. To go through the gate of Meridie Hardy's garden at the height of

the season is to enter a rosarian's dream and it would be hard, anywhere, to rival the

PREVIOUS PAGE: Roses all the way. 'Buff Beauty' and

overpowering impact of the rose-on-rose arrangements that meet the eye. Most of this rosy

'Sparrieshoop' illustrate the sheer flower power of these

drama lies between the front gate and front door of an imposing old suburban mansion

plantings, while *Aristea ecklonii, Lychnis coronaria,* and baby's

that stands on a corner block. The gate is bordered outside by austere, clipped-ivy covered

tears (*Erigeron karvinskianus*) screen their skirts. The roses

fences and framed on the inside by equally severe low box hedges. Two sides of the large

look fluffier, fuller and more fragile when set off by the

grassed front garden have been given a deep backdrop of greenery. Here a huge palm,

solid underplanting of spiky leaves.

a willow myrtle (*Agonis flexuosa*), a liquidambar (*L. styraciflua*), camellias, hydrangeas, philadelphus, *Murraya paniculata* and *Pittosporum* 'Silver Queen' embrace the wide area of mown grass. At ground level clivias, crinums, acanthus and agapanthus give the planting a strong finish.

On the lawn stand a venerable ash (*Fraxinus excelsior*) and an elegant crepe myrtle (*Lagerstroemia indica*). The plantings achieve their essential purpose—the elegant provision of privacy and shelter. In the rose season they also throw the eye to the spectacular bed on the other side of the path and to the front of the rose-bedecked house. Here *Rosa* 'Paul Transon', a rose with lax arching stems, neatly frames the front door with flat, apple-scented, coppery-pink flowers and plentiful shiny dark foliage. 'Buff Beauty' blows around the pillars while the low-growing, single, cluster-flowered 'Honeyflow', with its just off-white flowers, and the creamy-apricot 'Carabella' (both Australian bred Riethmuller roses) froth about at ground level.

Wild iris (*Dietes grandiflora*) and deep purple *Verbena bonariensis* dance on thread-like stalks through the mounding roses and are valued for the way in which they enhance the roses and for the colour they provide when the roses are not in flower. Box (*Buxus sempervirens*), a pale-blue kingfisher daisy (*Felicia bergeriana*), *Globularia cordifolia* with its lavender-blue, daisy-like pom-pom flowers, purple *Verbena erinoides* and French lavender (*Lavandula dentata*) provide solid mass—essential when winter leaves bare stems and empty spaces. (Even if Pemberton's 'Penelope' is there with her decorative, brilliant, winter-held hips.) And all fit nicely with the sophisticated, nicely balanced, apricot, copper, frail-pink, purple and lavender colour scheme that sets off the sandstone colour of the house. These other plants help eliminate any hint of the splotchy 'currants-on-a-bun' effect, often seen when roses are massed together. As do the clustered Rietmuller roses, which smother themselves in such solid masses of clustering frothing bloom that they never look blobby.

When the roses bloom, the great rose-filled bed that lies along the open side of the front garden is so flower-filled and rose-happy that it cannot fail to dominate the garden. However, it has been planted with the same attention to cohesion and form for all seasons as the rest of the garden. Again 'Buff Beauty' lends her unbeatable flowery presence and, on this occasion, performs as a flowering backdrop to the rich rose-embroidered tapestry, providing a visual link between the rose bed and the roses in front of the house. (A home-made, purpose-designed pruning device has been developed to keep this rose tidy and in its place.)

During the warmer months the roses call the fanfare, but well-chosen shrubs, bulbs and perennials are present to carry the music through all seasons. The misnamed white diosma (*Coleonema album*) forms a neat feathery hump, wormwood (*Artemisia arborescens*) provides lacy silvery foliage, a spiderwort (*Tradescantia* 'Purple Dome') provides a hump of spiky foliage and wealth of deep purple-blue flowers, while hellebores provide winter flowers and solid ground-level greenery. Meridie does not favour native Australian plants, but uses the South African *Aristea ecklonii* to great effect in this bed. And in the full blast of summer, when some roses lose their breath, the gaura (*Gaura lindheimeri*) 'goes mad' and rose-red hollyhocks reach for the sky.

But roses are what this spectacular bed is for and about, and the colours displayed here are, generally speaking, stronger than those used in front of the house. The two-tone pink 'Duet' puts on a spectacular and reliable show, as it often does in a hot climate, and repeats all through the summer months. 'Sparrieshoop' throws truss upon truss of scented apple-blossom pink flowers. The freely blooming 'Clair Matin' adds glowing pink petals, golden stamens, cocoa-coloured stems and dark leaves. The glowing 'Radox Bouquet' adds a fairly constant supply of pure-pink petals. (The rose finds favour with its owner, but like many other gardeners, she complains about 'that terrible name'.) Yellow is provided by 'Graham Thomas' and 'Friesia' (syn. 'Korresia' and 'Sunsprite') which provide petals in plenty over long periods—and that is what this garden is about.

Behind the house lies a swimming pool and the child-protecting wire fences have been giving a second purpose—they support roses. Here 'Gold Bunny' is regarded as a star performer, with the picked blooms lasting for about two weeks in a vase—and that is without resorting to the burning of stems. In the reflected light and heat 'Kathleen Harrop' loses the wet-and-weary appearance she often displays in cooler, wetter climates and flounces about with enormous prettiness, while the very fragrant 'Francis E. Lester' displays a wealth of tiny pink buds and a festoon of flowers. Interestingly, in this garden, 'Iceberg' displays distinctly pink petals when grown close to the pool—not just the odd pink-tinted petal but an over-whelmingly pink impression.

Roses are what this garden is about and here, in Australia's rose capital, they are well chosen for a long, dramatic and colourful display. They are also well grown, well placed, well arranged and well trained. The results speak for themselves, while the care given to the companion plantings means that this garden never looks like anything other than what it is—the private garden of a well-informed, passionate lover of the rose.

OPPOSITE TOP, LEFT TO RIGHT: 'Buff Beauty', an English-bred shrub rose, covers the verandah; 'Radox Bouquet', a fragrant, cluster-flowered floribunda, displays another perfect bloom. CENTRE, LEFT TO RIGHT: *Aristea ecklonii* provides a foil for 'Radox Bouquet'; The lax, arching stems of the French-bred, apple-scented rose, 'Paul Transon'. After a magnificent first flush, it continues to flower lustily throughout the summer. BOTTOM, LEFT TO RIGHT: On the ground, beneath 'Buff Beauty', the Australian-bred Riethmuller rose 'Honeyflow' flowers from mid-spring to late autumn; a friend of the family.

OFTEN A GREAT GARDEN is dismissed with the comment that its creator is blessed

with an artist's eye. And the comment does indeed describe Diana Morgan's talents, but

when faced with the reality of this small courtyard garden in the suburbs of Melbourne,

Victoria, it sounds weak. It dismisses, for example, the persistent, methodical approach

of a true collector and an extensive knowledge built through years of detailed observation

and investigation. Nevertheless, it is the eye of the artist that gives the place its creative

edge. In design and arrangement it avoids relying on any recognised style, culture,

colour combination or plant campanionships. Modern sculpture and craft sit beside

older pieces, containers from junk shops keep company with those of more illustrious

pedigrees, and an important collection of succulents shares space with an equally

important collection of old-fashioned roses. If handled with less authority, the mix could

easily look eccentric, affected or quaint. As it is, nothing looks out of place.

PREVIOUS PAGE: The flowers of the Mexican Echeveria pilosa seen in the dawn light. OPPOSITE: Container-grown succulents are carefully grouped in such a way that the many different shapes, forms and textures never look messy, awkward or quaint. Rosa banksiae 'Alba Plena', the only scented one of its kind, cascades over Echeveria superbum and E. 'Cinderella'.

Diana describes the garden she took on in 1966 as being a 'typical old lady's front garden'. The site was open to the road and displayed a hedge of 'Lorraine Lee' roses, fiddly lavender-filled beds, crazy paving and a certain amount of dust. Clearly, a new look and a more practical approach to the use of precious and limited space were in order.

Garden pictures that appealed were cut from a wide variety of magazines. On inspection, they revealed to the then novice gardener that texture, leaf, form, shape, sculpture, proportion, colour and the balance between these elements were of greater interest to her than the flowers she thought to be her first consideration.

Diana's husband, Nigel, transformed the space by designing a courtyard using old bricks for the enclosing walls and paving. These now provide a pleasantly uniform backdrop to the plants and garden artefacts.

The old-fashioned roses were Diana's first great plant interest (she founded the Victorian branch of the Heritage Rose Society), and from roses she learnt the important lesson of sticking with climate-suitable plants. Only roses that maintain good health without undue attention and those whose human-hungry prickles can be placed above head height, have been retained today. Importantly, the selection ensures a lengthy and varied display of bloom.

The season begins in October with a foaming display from *Rosa banksiae* 'Alba Plena'—the only scented banksia rose. This climbing plant has been trained so that the stems look like sculptured pieces of twisted wood at ground level, while the flowery performance billows out well above the level of the human head. Three bourbon roses display their flowers simultaneously in November: 'Souvenir de la Malmaison' begins its long display of soft pink petals, 'Gloire de Dijon' showers the place with pale buff-yellow petals, and 'Variegata di Bologna', a speckled striped crimson-and-white curiosity, provides both focus and contrast. After which the climbing ramblers 'Seafoam' and 'Lamarque' join the centuries of rose breeding and present their flowers. The evergreen *Rosa bracteata* has retained its place too. Good health, evergreen leaves and four months of cascading, clean-white flowers earn this rose top marks, but its potential size and vigour necessitate fierce control—and in this garden that is what it gets.

Succulents also answered the need for plants that would withstand the rigours of family life and survive the owner's occasional absence. Moreover, their varied textures, colours, shapes and formations appealed to Diana's discerning eye. (Incidentally, Diana suggests that succulents have been out of fashion for as long as they have because, unlike other plants, they do not die when left untended. They survive but sit about looking unspeakably tatty.)

Well-groomed succulents, each in a container chosen to suit its particular characteristics, are grouped on tables, by the gate, and in focal positions by the front door or below windows. Often their placement is chosen so that at some point in the day their slightly translucent leaves will be caught in low rays of sunlight and acquire the magical hint of inner luminosity so characteristic of these plants. To the uninitiated, the leaf colours are amazing, and include reds, browns, purples, blacks, yellows, jade-greens, grey-greens, dark-greens, oranges and pinks.

Bowls are crammed with the round, rose-like tinted heads of *Echeveria* species. Their more colourful and curious cultivars, in a wide variety of shapes and shades, also find a place. The grey, leathery-looking leaves of *Graptopetalum paraguayense* flow over the sides of some containers and nearby *Sedum rubrotinctum* 'Aurora' snuggles its tiny leaves down in its pot and glows with the intensity of a coal fire. *Euphorbia myrsinites* and *Agave attenuata* provide grey-green sculptures, and varied forms of *Cotyledon orbiculata* add the intrigue of their crested shapes and margined leaves. The bronzed tree-like presence of *Kalanchoe beharensis* adds a curious upright shape to a mass of other curious shapes and subtle shades.

Each plant is labelled, and a record of its preferences and progress kept. This includes the times at which the leaf colour is at its most intense and when the flowers are likely to appear. Any plant that fails to look its best is quickly escorted to the back garden for a period of rest and recuperation. This gardener is adamant that succulents need the same attentions as any other garden plant if they are to look well groomed and attractive. She adds that growing plants in pots allows for individual soil mixes and helps hugely in 'the enjoyable process of creating varying and dramatic juxtapositions'. She also describes the collecting experience as being a solitary one that 'no-one can make for you', but one that can be 'shared with a million friends'.

Incidentally, no plant earns a place in this garden unless it is capable of providing some form of decoration for the house, and Diana is noted for her arrangements of leaves, seedpods, stems and flowers. She is also known for her quietly humorous approach to collecting and gardening, and revels in the name of the latest cultivar to join her succulent collection. It is called 'Cinderella', and has tiny red tips on its shoe-like leaves.

OPPOSITE TOP, LEFT TO RIGHT: *Graptopetalum paraguayense* with dew drop; *Sempervivum arachnoideum* inhabits a mallee root. BOTTOM, LEFT TO RIGHT: *Aloe plicatilis* guards an arrangement of *Aeonium tricolour*, an *Echeveria* species housed in an ikebana vase and *E.* 'Princess Anne'; *E. elegans* in an Indian brass container.

IMPRES

SUBURBAN TRAFFIC, with its constant throbbing hum and occasional honk, churns past the high brick walls of The Mosaic Garden. The house itself, a converted red-brick church hall, is nicely proportioned, but hardly of landmark status. A large camphor laurel tree (*Cinnamomum camphora*), a lemon-scented gum (*Corymbia citriodora* syn. *Eucalyptus citriodora*) and well-grown banana trees (*Musa* species)—all fairly common in frost-free inner Melbourne—can be seen from the street. The suggestion is of a small, shady, ordinary suburban garden. Only the glimpse of a huge prickly pear (*Opuntia vulgaris*) sitting on a roof and the notice set in the wall indicate anything to the contrary.

Yet within these walls everything surprises, entrances and fascinates. Another world has been found. Size, space and location are immaterial. The sudden impact of the unexpected, glowing, shining colours, flickering in the ever-moving dappled light, attracts immediate attention. Thereafter, the detail and design, the colour combinations

PREVIOUS PAGE: The look of this richly embroidered 'tablecloth' belies a hard surface. OPPOSITE: A star fell from the sky on to a rock pushed up from the earth. The leaves of *Agave attenuata* give shelter and echo the sharp points of the star while the shape of the mushrooming rock is picked up by the surrounding pebbles.

and contrasts, the curves and flat surfaces, the illusions and interactions combine and contrive to hold the eye and entrance the senses.

Every view (and there are 'views' in this small self-contained space) is different, with each vista revealing different treatments and patterns, atmospheres and aspects, effects and impressions.

The Mosaic Garden, a work in progress, is the creation of Margot Knox, an artist renowned in her own right and widow of the acclaimed architect Alistair Knox. However, Margot always points out that her children play active and creative roles in the garden's development. Sophie Knox worked on and completed the high blue wall. Alexander Knox shaped and made the metal frames for the large vases and Alistair Knox Jnr forged the rounded iron gate, with the decorative ironwork being that of sculptor Jacki Staude, whose work Margot greatly admires.

When one examines the elements that make up this enchanted place, one realises how many different artistic and cultural influences have been brought together, and brought together in harmony, in the one small space. A wall here seems to owe something to Mexico.

Some plant and mosaic arrangements display a vaguely Californian influence, a tablecloth seems to have blown in from France and a wall been licked into shape by a rolling, frothing enamelled blue sea. A tiny pond implies untold depths, while a container suggests some fabulous fairytale plant. *Agave attenuata* never looked more attenuated or more at home than it does in this garden, where its mosaic encrusted container adds and combines with its particular persona. It is as if the plant and its container have emerged together from some half-remembered fairytale by the brothers Grimm.

Whatever the cultural influences and references, everything here seems larger than life. Light spaces seem larger and brighter than is usual, the shaded spaces more mysterious, and the created atmospheres more intense.

No pond ever looked wetter or deeper than the tiny pond, its rim brightly encrusted in enamelled green and set off with green glowing 'rocks' resembling fantastic lily pads. (The green is an exact match to the emerald-green moss growing on the back of the dodo-like bird that does duty as a fountain.) Black-stemmed, dark-leaved *Alocasia amazonica* and the smaller white calla lily (*Zantedeschia aethiopica* var. *childsiana*) with their paddle-shaped leaves extend the watery atmosphere.

No roofline ever looked more in tune with the sky than this stepped roofline decorated with pots of *Aloe arborescens*. The pots (Chinese copies of an Italian design) were chosen after a long parade of exchanges and improvements. When the right pots were found they were glued down for safety and filled with sand to slow the plants' growth.

No table ever looked more inviting than the one with its ever-ready mosaic tablecloth. (The work on this piece is fine and tightly detailed. The impression is light, airy, lace-like, ready to blow away, and of the Impressionists.) And no house ever nestled more comfortably into its garden than this one does. The two make perfect and inseparable companions.

In this self-contained world the senses are given extravagant treats. Plants are chosen, placed and nurtured with careful expertise,

ABOVE: Matched pots containing *Aloe arborescens* stand in silhouette along a stepped, mosaic-clad roofline.

and the contribution they make to the garden is as important as that of the mosaics. A light leaf canopy defines much of the place. In the dappled flickering light beneath it, plants with reed-like foliage—dianellas, dietes, clivias, crinums, strelitzias and cordylines—add sharp shapes and elongated shadows. In light sun-bright corners, light-loving succulents, each in its perfectly chosen pot, are crowded together and, adding light to light, given brilliant backdrops.

For Margot, inanimate objects and plants both have strong human-like personalities. They amuse, they entertain, they influence and they irritate. Margot observes and cherishes them all—and puts them to work in her other-worldly world. The camphor laurel, which sheds what Margot calls 'ratbag leaves' is nevertheless honoured with the creation of a table which looks all the more enchanting for a sprinkling of the ever-falling small, crisp, russet leaves. A row of white mosaic pots (Margot observes that cheap white Italian china has a wonderful deep glossy-glaze) 'make sense in this garden'. Red china flowers placed in relief on a glossy smooth brilliant backdrop of ceramic 'pull things together and stop it looking like a lunatic's playground.'

Birds are here too—in real life and in ceramic form. A very jolly-looking parrot perches permanently between two pots, while two china chicken heads peer from a container like loony old broody biddies.

The huge banana trees (in many gardens of this size these would look too big, dominant and top-heavy) are called 'mad trees', and are quite clearly loved for their sculptural brand of 'madness'.

A particular shade of turquoise 'lifts everything', an acid green 'goes well with everything', blue and white combinations 'are energising' and that 'funny old pink' resolves problems.

Margot stresses that her chosen medium, namely mosaic, demands much more of a craftsman than a couple of spare hours, broken plates and glue. There is always, for example, a loose design in her head before she begins, and she stresses the necessity of exercising control over the design and medium and of 'grinding things into shape'. And she knows her medium. Gutsy colours taken from old tiles are used to

ABOVE: Garden forms of *Ranunculus asiaticus* stand on an arrangement of old glazed tiles.

great effect in gutsy arrangements. (Margot remarks on their 'inner glow' and suggests that the lead used in old glazes may account for it.) But when a fine lacy effect is required, then small pieces of translucent French porcelain are employed. Each piece is carefully cut, not casually broken. This adds to the fascination, as close inspection often reveals a tiny flower, a face, a painted leaf, bird or petal. All have become part of some bigger picture but are, in themselves, entire, isolated and intriguing. Nothing is placed at random. Each piece must be exactly right for its place and purpose. And each design and theme must sit happily with its immediate surroundings and with the whole garden.

In conclusion, Margot says 'I've come to like broken things more than entire things. They make things.' (As she prepares for her next exhibition of paintings, she is planning a mosaic bib for a Staffordshire dog with a hole in its chest.) She also speaks frankly of the medium itself, calling it 'suspect' and 'over the top', and is the first to say that 'the line between highly decorative and kitsch is very fine indeed'.

Whatever her concerns, the garden is now well recognised as an artistic work of great merit and originality. And when it is opened to the public, thousands of visitors—teachers and students, artists and craftspeople, gardeners and gapers, locals and foreigners—make their way to the unobtrusive garden gate and stay within the high walls for unexpected lengths of time.

BELOW: A barley-twist column carries a garlanded pot filled with spiky *Aloe vera*. OPPOSITE: A detail of the mosaic tablecloth with its scattering of camphor laurel (*Cinnamomum camphora*) leaves and floral centrepiece.

TO MAKE—FROM SCRATCH—a large country garden in a fairly isolated area,

requires more vision, discipline and tenacity than many of us possess. All too often plant

enthusiasts fall for the 'topsy' school-of-design and push fences outwards, bit by bit,

every time they feel a need for more space and more plants. And bit by bit, the site

loses cohesion and all relationship with the surrounding landscape—sometimes even

whatever it was that first drew the enthusiast to the place is destroyed. Happily, none of

PREVIOUS PAGE: White watsonia (*W. borbonica* subsp.

this has happened at Roskhill in the hills outside Adelaide. The house, sited just below

ardernei), kangaroo paws, *Anigozanthos* species and

the brow of a low wind-protecting hill, enjoys a ninety-degree aspect over a rural valley

Jerusalem sage (*Phlomis fruticosa*) separate the garden

of exceptional beauty. The ornamental garden which both separates and ties the house

from well-treed paddocks. OPPOSITE: The Japanese rose,

and surrounding landscape together, takes its inspiration and scale from the topography

'Nozomi'—usually listed as a climber—also performs well

of this wondrous place with its vast skyscape, wide, wrapping horizon and rolling rural

as a tumbler. Here it tumbles over a rock embankment.

aspect. The garden, begun in 1971, sits easily on its site, enhancing rather than distracting

from a strong spirit of place. Its creation and maintenance have been a joint effort between Alan and Skye McGregor—with each belittling their own efforts and commending the efforts of the other!

It took 110 loads of landfill (gleaned free of charge from local road workings) to form the plateau which now sits on two sides of the house. This grassed, carefully sculpted area looks like an integral part of the site and pushes the eye onward and outward towards the valley. A huge, steep, wide, boomerang-shaped bank-bed edges the far side of this lawn. In the 'elbow' a group of lemon-scented gums (*Corymbia citriodora* syn. *Eucalyptus citriodora*) add the emphasis of their lovely, hanging silhouette to the drop in the land, to the shape of the site and the power of the place.

The bank is generously planted with a mix of native and exotic plants. Mounding forms and misty effects are used to offset the all-important gums and the magical view. The scale is huge, and no attempt is made to minimise it or 'fuss it up'. Shrubs are wide and spreading. Members of the same species are often grouped together—an arrangement that suits both the wide horizon and the fact that this bed is not only on view from the house but also from all sides and from several levels.

Leptospermum juniperinum 'Horizontalis' makes an outstanding contribution with its dense, dark, arching foliage and thick snow of white springtime flowers. (It probably also contributes to the happy habitat this garden provides for the electric-blue wrens whose skittish behaviour is part of the garden's persona.) *Westringia fruticosa* 'Smokie' is grouped in mounding, misty patches. Whitish variegations on greyish leaves are permitted; so are silver-grey and blue-green leaves. Chrome-yellow variegations and sharp yellow-greens are hardly used at all, or are handled with great sensitivity. *Correa* species fan out across the ground, keeping the weeds down, the birds safe and fed, and the lovers of elegant winter-borne flowers content. *Cistus* species and white daisy bushes (*Argyranthemum frutescens*) provide some more mounding shapes and sparkling flowers.

Annuals, perennials and bulbs are used too—either planted in large patches or, if their nature and appearance suit the scene, allowed to appear where they will provide uniformity and cohesion while in flower, only to be reined in quickly once flowering ceases. The Chinese forget-me-not (*Cynoglossum amabile*) is planted in a large, single, striking patch. (The common forget-me-not (*Myosotis sylvatica*) is not thought to have what it takes in this strong scene.) The violet larkspur (*Delphinium peregrinum*) and Queen Ann's lace (*Anthriscus sylvestris*) provide tall, shimmering, misting flowers in mid-spring. A group of alliums (*Allium giganteum*) add intriguing Russian-cupola buds and purple flowers. White *Gladiolus* x *colvillei* 'The Bride' and white chincherinchees (*Ornithogalum thyrsoides*) are planted in large patches and set against a backdrop of the spreading blue-flowered *Ceanothus griseus* var. *horizontalis*. Saltbush (*Atriplex cinerea*), spoken of by Skye as 'a good filler plant', makes a somewhat surprising addition to an ornamental garden, but the plant has what it takes in these exposed surroundings and looks elegant in a cultivated garden.

Below the big bed lies a wide mown ride. A pleasant strip planting on the far side separates the garden from the tree-sprinkled paddock. Much of this separating strip is planted with Australian native plants. (The initial plantings at Roskhill were, primarily, of native plants. Since then some experimentation with and enjoyment of exotic plants has taken place, but today, as and when replanting is necessary, native plants are usually chosen, with preference being given to those bearing small flowers.) *Thryptomene* species do well here and *Melaleuca incana* 'Velvet Cushion' provides dense, soft grey-green foliage, pale lemony flowers and bird habitat. *Leptospermum* 'Ruby Glow', with its dark foliage and ruby-red flowers, makes a splendid colour companion to a callistemon bearing small scarlet flowers.

On the higher side of the house, the mown grass swells out and is surrounded by a deep, largely exotic planting. (The garden, which stands on solid clay, has been built up and the soil broken down with many a thick mulch of organic material. And what was once a difficult growing medium has become friable, rich, water retentive and super-successful—with the amazing mass of apricot flowers from *Leucospermum cordifolium* proving the point.)

A frothing European elder (*Sambucus nigra*, bought under the name of 'perennial Queen Anne's Lace'!) stands at the far end while, to one side, the port wine magnolia (*Michelia figo* syn. *fuscata*) scents the air. A discreet stepping stone path leads through perennials, bulbs and shrubs to a secluded seat. The idea in this open, all-welcoming, all-seen garden, was to provide a place where proposals could be made in private, but so far, none of the young have taken advantage of this thoughtful provision. However, the seat is in regular use by those wanting to get away from it all for a moment or two, and there they can sit surrounded by flowers and look out over the golden valley. The black kangaroo paw (*Macropidia fuliginosa*), which many find a short-term challenge ending in failure, grows and flowers well here, making an effective and unusual companion to a yellow daylily (*Hemerocallis* sp.).

This elegant, spidery daylily finds favour in this garden owner's eyes; many of the fat, fulsome modern cultivars do not.

At the lower side of the garden, a pergola made from beams taken from an old wool store and covered in jasmine (*Jasminum azoricum*) leads to a tennis court that has been cut into the hill. Here plants which flower in summer are given preference, and an outstanding flowery mix of the pale pink and white *Rosa* 'Nozomi' and the blue *Convolvulus sabatius* tumbles over glowing, golden granite rocks. Above them, the white form of the evergreen bluebell creeper (*Sollya heterophylla*) romps about.

The garden is full of pretty, unusual plantings. White watsonia (*W. borbonica* subsp. *ardernei*) grows with kangaroo paws; the intense blue of the starry Chinese forget-me-not sits close to the acid yellows of euphorbias; the evergreen, white-flowered perennial candytuft (*Iberis sempervirens*) glistens near the delightful little *Rosa* 'Moonsprite'; a coppery berberis is used near a dark-leaf pink-flowered leptospermum and an upright yellow iris grows near a mound of yellow Jerusalem Sage (*Phlomis fruticosa*). Elsewhere this phlomis is used with the yellow geum (*Geum chiloense* 'Lady Stratheden'). The sugar-pink *Rosa* 'Radio Times' blooms nearby. And white borage (*Borago officinalis* 'Alba') softens the many blobby effects achieved by *Rosa* 'Iceberg'.

In this large country garden the designer knows exactly when and how to strike a strong note, when to go for some pretty embellishment and when to let it flow. It's a highly musical garden. The land itself carries the main tune, but the owners know how to decorate, embellish and emphasise. More importantly, they know when to leave well alone and let the land speak for itself.

RICH SOIL AND PLENTIFUL RAIN have contributed to the making of several

noted gardens in the Southern Highlands of New South Wales. However, there are

few that combine a great Victorian inheritance with creativity in the modern idiom.

Few which have had the benefit of several renowned designers, plantsmen, architects

and sculptors. And still fewer that are superbly maintained today. In these respects

Retford Park stands alone. Samuel Hordern built his Italianate mansion in 1887 and

surrounded it with a park and noted arboretum. Botanical collections were fashionable

at that time, but many of those setting up estates appear to have bought their trees as

job lots. Most probably, these ready-made collections consisted of little more than a

few oaks, some everlasting evergreens, a monkey puzzle (*Araucaria araucana*) that died

and a weeping willow (*Salix babylonica*), propagated from cuttings taken from

Napoleon's tomb on St Helena, which subsequently invaded local watercourses.

Happily, at Retford Park the evidence suggests that the tree plantings did more to set rather than follow fashion, and that the selection was based on real knowledge and the instincts of a true collector with a magnificent vision for the future. Today the imposing house—which must have looked sadly out of scale with the surrounding landscape at first—sits lightly on the site, its glory enhanced by towering trees, a great wealth of foliage and a well-treed park.

Beside the house stands one of the finest bunya bunya pines (*Araucaria bidwillii*) to be found outside the tree's native Queensland. On the other side, a mature pin oak (*Quercus palustris*) and a great bull bay magnolia (*Magnolia grandiflora*) stand guard. Making an impressive backdrop to the view from the house, a giant redwood (*Sequoiadendron giganteum*), which is indeed a giant, stands with an equally large Monterey cypress (*Cupressus macrocarpa*) and a Himalayan cedar (*Cedrus deodara*). A huge and handsome Caucasian fir (*Abies nordmanniana*) displays its ground-kissing green glory while Algerian oaks (*Quercus canariensis*) rise to great heights and have, with full maturity, acquired the wonderful domed tops for which they are famed. All these trees are now fully mature and provide great curtains and blankets of solid greenery.

In 1964 Retford Park was acquired by James Fairfax AO, the philanthropist, noted patron of the arts and past Chairman of the

BELOW: The Millennium Canal, where water and mown grass merge. Here twenty young ginkgo trees (*G. biloba*) link a disciplined design to the more random plantings of a previous generation.

former family-owned media company, John Fairfax Ltd. It was James who took on the task of revitalising the tree collection, preserving all that is worthy from the past and enhancing the garden with new and different decorative elements.

Overgrown senescent trees (mainly conifers) were removed, giving the garden a lighter, more spacious atmosphere. Deciduous trees were pruned, shaped, cleaned of dead wood and made safe, and today the noted oak collection gives the garden much of its summertime leafy feeling. And the great cherry laurel (*Prunus laurocerasus*) hedges that give necessary definition to the different garden compartments stand thick, solid, glossy and stout against the mountain winds.

More trees have been planted, and red-flowering horse chestnuts (*Aesculus* x *carnea*) are now large enough to add a unifying flounce of frothy flowers to some parts of the old garden. Near the house, a tricolor beech (*Fagus sylvatica* 'Purpurea Tricolor') is making strong progress and will, in time, carry the leafy theme onwards as other, now mature trees, begin their decline. When large enough to set off the pink walls of the house, the pink-purple leaves will make much

ABOVE: An alder (*Alnus glutinosa*) enjoys the gentle autumnal sunlight. A pin oak (*Quercus palustris*) stands behind, while to the right of the drive a purple-leaf plum (*Prunus cerasifera* 'Nigra') adds deep colour. Branches of the golden cypress (*Cupressus macrocarpa* 'Lambertiana Aurea') hang above, adding a hint of shadowy drama.

more than a pretty statement. Dogwoods (*Cornus florida* and *C. capitata*) are particularly impressive and magnolias now flourish and flower beneath the massive trees of the earlier plantings.

As often happens when connoisseurs search for quality rather than known names, a well-grown bushy dogwood has, so far, failed to find a precise nomenclature. And by a side gate, a nameless Japanese maple cultivar (*Acer palmatum*) has grown to an unusual size and displays peculiarly bright reddish foliage throughout the year.

The late John Codrington, a noted English landscape designer, was responsible for the unusual and amusing arrangement immediately in front of the house. There the turning circle, instead of sporting the traditional mown grass and single central tree, has been given a central path leading to a fountain. Deep beds border the path and bulge with silver-grey foliage. Shrubby plants like *Teucrium fruticans*, wormwood (*Artemisia arborescens*) and French lavender (*Lavandula dentata*), all of which are periodically cut into great domes, are used to great effect. Blue and white agapanthus, yellow-flowering Jerusalem sage (*Phlomis fruticosa*) and a spreading, white and blue daisy-flowered cultivar of *Osteospermum fruticosum* add a little piquant colour. The fountain itself is set off with paired trees—Italian cypresses (*Cupressus sempervirens* 'Stricta'), *Acer platanoides* 'Crimson King' and rare coffin junipers (*Juniperus recurva*) form a happy link to the surrounding curtain of foliage.

A knot garden, the work of David Wilkinson (an architect whose ongoing contribution to the modern garden has been considerable) stands to one side of the house. The scale is huge and in proportion to the mansion the garden serves. Here, the rococo reproduction furbelows and flounces popular in late 20th century suburban gardens have been rejected in favour of a design of considerable originality and strength. Square-cut hip-high hedges are arranged in an intricate straight line pattern. All angles are at ninety degrees. *Teucrium fruticans* and two forms of *Buxus sempervirens* have been employed and, with their current maturity and superb maintenance, now achieve the status of a three dimensional, hard-edged work of art. Ten mop-top robinias (*Robinia pseudoacacia* 'Inermis') add height, while their pleasant ferny mobility softens the strong architecture of the hedges and house. The huge climbing rose 'Albertine' and the clinging climbing hydrangea (*Hydrangea petiolaris*) are set against the house and, in season, add dramatic torrents of flower.

Screened from the area immediately visible from the house are a series of large rectangular self-contained gardens. Each has a different character and all are separated, one from the other, by the dense, high, thick cherry laurel hedges.

OPPOSITE TOP: Stone dogs guard the front entry while *Cupressus torulosa*, *Amelanchier canadensis* and *Tilia* 'Petiolaris' guard the dogs. *Teucrium fruticans* has been given a well-rounded clip while *Artemisia arborescens* still hangs loose. OPPOSITE BELOW LEFT: One of the many enticing views into the park. OPPOSITE BELOW RIGHT: A 'Petal Chair' made by Jonathan McCord from the native scrub-rosewood (*Dysoxylium fraseranum*) and old fencing wire. ABOVE: An unknown mythical figure adds a note of antiquity.

An Emu Walk has been laid out at the highest level, where the park's flock can be viewed as they make their stately procession through a series of interlinked paths defined by stilt hedges concocted from linden trees (*Tilia cordata*). Beside and below the Emu Walk lies the Green Room. Once a yard for hens, ducks and geese, this large, mown, open, laurel-enclosed space now provides repose for both the eye and spirit. The sculpture 'Euphoric Angels' by Inge King stands at its centre. (It is not, however, a particularly quiet space. Birds—both those in the nearby aviaries and the native birds that whistle through the sky or screech from the tree tops—see to that.)

The third hedged room, once a tennis court, now holds the Red Border on one side and on the other a row of *Prunus serrulata* 'Kanzan', whose sudsy froth of pink spring blossom is followed by the drooping racemes of laburnum species that grow alongside. Small-flowered, big-clustered, rambling, grey-purple roses—'Veilchenblau' (1909), 'Rose-Marie Viaud' (1924) and a Banksia rose, all somewhat neglected by modern gardeners—hang in great festoons from the wire netting that once enclosed the court. Their dusty shades sit well with the Persian carpet colours of the border; reds, purples and burgundies with touches of sugar-pink and lemon-yellow. The fourth garden is the famous pool garden, created by the late Guilford Bell.

Beside the two kilometre-long drive, with its edging of huge pines (*Pinus radiata*), Russian olives (*Elaeagnus angustifolia*) and park-like arboretum, lies the most recent addition to the garden—the Millennium Canal. Here mown grass meets the water's edge with scarcely a seam. (In the words of David Wilkinson, its designer, the effect is 'drop dead modern'.) The water surface itself, in a pretty conceit, is ten metres wide and two hundred metres long—making, in all, two thousand square metres of shining water. Even prettier was the idea of setting it off with acid-green, ferny ginkgos (*Ginkgo biloba*)—a species that dates from the Jurassic and Cretaceous periods and is possibly the oldest living tree species on the planet.

Today the garden of Retford Park summarises much that has taken place in the past hundred years of gardening in Australia, and it has joined the 21st century in great style. Nothing here sinks into a pastiche of styles past or into irritating imitative trendiness.

This garden has been lucky to fall into good hands, most particularly those of James Fairfax AO. Those who have the chance to wander through it are also in luck, as it is an experience that can be taken at several levels. It can be taken simply as an undemanding, enjoyable wander through pleasant surroundings, or as lessons in botany, scale and proportion, decoration and the disciplined lack of it, and in garden design at its highest manifestations.

OPPOSITE: The famous pool garden is the work of the renowned architect, Guilford Bell. Here his pavilion seems to float between a real sky and a water-reflected sky, between solid glossy-green hedges and the faded shades of an open rolling landscape, between the past and tomorrow.

AT EVANDALE, THE TASMANIAN GARDEN of Tim and Julie Barbour,

horticultural skills and plant management are taken to high levels, and the sophisticated

results are used to enhance an exceptional site. Close to the pretty Victorian house,

stylistically appropriate formal arrangements are set out geometrically on level ground—

the front door is framed, a terrace given a formal parterre, paths edged with low clipped

hedging and an orchard given a small but formal apple-embraced walk. The spaces are

clearly designated and boldly designed. They serve and suit the house well, echoing and

enlarging its lines and proportions, giving the buildings appropriately decorative settings

and displaying the successful refinements in plant training for which this garden is noted.

Box (*Buxus sempervirens*) and *Lonicera nitida* are used extensively as low hedging with

Euonymus fortunei 'Emerald Gaiety' and *E. fortunei* 'Emerald and Gold' adding

colour to the dark, defining, evergreen outlines. Height is added in the traditional

manner, with plants grown as standards and clipped into perfect lollipop shapes. Sometimes the 'trunks' are twined around stakes. Sometimes they stand alone, straight and strong. The sweet bay (*Laurus nobilis*) is used to great effect, but so are several plants not normally associated with presentation in the standard form. For example, blue-flowered ceanothus species, escallonias and the shrubby germander (*Teucrium fruticans*) are all used to add height and ball-like shapes to the square-cut low-growing hedging plants.

Apple trees have been espaliered precisely and, in some instances, the branches grafted, with each leader devoted to a different variety. Rather than spacing the branches close together and holding the eye within the walk, they are widely spaced and allow a view into a small orchard. It is a clever contrivance and typical of this garden's design, where the tricky task of marrying formal and informal elements is met with such an easy success that the transition is almost imperceptible.

As the garden spreads away from the house, the design softens. Beds have curved edges and flow with the increasing slope of the land.

Strong forms are set against fluffy frailer ones. Mown grass swirls like water through fluffy ornamental grasses.

Single plantings too marry the formal to the informal. For example, honey locusts (*Gleditsia triacanthos* f. *inermis*) rise from within clipped lonicera hedges, adding a row of straight trunks to the formal planting and a joyous feathery frill of topknots to the informal and rural elements. (And they add amusement to bare branches in winter with their huge black pods and windy rattles.)

As levelled surfaces give way to natural slopes, elements of previous gardens are incorporated into the design. A stately horse chestnut (*Aesculus hippocastanum*) stands in its own grassed glade. Great dead trunks of Monterey cypress (*Cupressus macrocarpa*)—stoic relics of an old shelter-belt—remain and give the garden an air of constancy as they frame an old gate.

In summer the strong designs are softened with plants of a more dancing, mobile habit. Curved beds gain softer curves but greater presence with thick swathes of ornamental grass. Great ribbons of ornamental grasses (*Deschampsia caespitosa* and *Carex morrowii*) are used to frame the view to the river, with the water and seed heads glinting in the summer sun. *Gaura lindheimeri* holds a myriad of light, bright, butterfly flowers on long thin stems and the fluttering dance goes on all through the summer months. A soft-looking lavender (*Lavandula stoechas*), which flowers over a long period, makes a softly mounding hedge separating the dark colors and strong geometric shapes of the formal entry area from the softer shapes and colours of the rolling paddocks. At the front of the house, frothing humps of catmint (*Nepeta faassenii*) make happy companions to the thrusting hybrid roses. It is a time-honoured arrangement, but here, instead of the catmint edging the bed and separating path from bed, it is placed behind the roses and against the wall of the house. As a result, the often ugly seam between house and soil is lost in grey-green fluffy foliage and the dry under-eve area is utilised. It's an interesting tweak to a traditional arrangement and suits both the age and architecture of the house.

The designs and plantings throughout this garden are both decorative and strong, and are arranged to serve both the house and the view beyond the garden. Trees add emphasis to the intrinsic elements of the site. They are not used to terminate views or form visual blockades. The trained and grafted plants are used for decoration rather than to create self-contained space. And, as one looks from the garden towards the open countryside or towards the enchanting valley of the South Esk River where church spires rise from clumping trees, there are no man-made focal points. The countryside itself is given an important priority here—and this garden serves that importance.

OPPOSITE TOP, LEFT TO RIGHT: The column-like stem of *Echium wildpretii*; A multi-graft apple tree, exquisitely espaliered. OPPOSITE BOTTOM, LEFT TO RIGHT: Apple blossom from 'The Apple Island'; Venerable Monterey cypresses (*Cupressus macrocarpa*), probably planted for the purpose of shelter, now dwarf an old gate.

THE VAST FLAT PLAINS THAT LINK Victoria and South Australia are broken by

abrupt lumps, bumps, hills and mountains—the leftovers of long-extinct volcanoes.

The inland climate is harsh, with cold winters, hot summers, spasmodic rainfall and

legendary winds. Wigandia, with its one and a half hectare garden, is set on one of the

bump-top sites, with the garden taking the best and worst of this challenging climate—

and making the very best of it. Once, when Australia was said to ride on the sheep's

back, the area was enviably prosperous. Great fortunes were made, great houses built

and great gardens put in place. The estates of Europe were re-created—many to

crumble within a couple of generations with the fall in the price of wool. However, one

of the first things William Martin, creator of the garden of Wigandia, says is that he

doesn't concur with the replication of old world garden culture in the colonies and much

prefers the unique work of Guilfoyle—particularly his blend of old and new world floras.

(William Guilfoyle was the 19th century director and principal designer of the renowned Royal Botanic Gardens in Melbourne. He also did private work in several grand, extensive local gardens. Some have survived and are held in high regard today.)

The latter is evident at a glance but, in some ways, the garden owes as much to the district's prosperous past as it does to the climate and local topography. Corrugated iron—a utilitarian, transportable material once much used in rural Australia (and frequently put to use in the unseen nether quarters of the great brick and stone mansions of the area)—is used extensively in the garden. But here it gains a new persona and is used as an up-front ornamental fabric. A curvaceous iron-scaled snake basks on open ground. Sculptural 'pot plants' are created from this undulating iron. Large gates in impressive decorative settings welcome the visitor. In shape and scale these gates are reminiscent of the grandiose arrangements that often herald an estate of social importance. But, being made of corrugated iron, the effect is entertainingly different. One sculptural arrangement is actually called 'Lysaght's Colonial Revenge'. The reference being to the well-known manufacturers of these galvanised corrugated iron sheets—their stamp in the middle of one 'wall' is clearly visible. Magnificent rusting iron boilers

(relics of the wool industry) have been salvaged from old estates, and are now put to new purposes. Some are used right side up as plant containers. (The combination of rusty-red iron curves and the straight, narrow, rust-striped stems of *Miscanthus sinensis* 'Zebrinus' is particularly effective.) Others are placed upside down with their perfectly rounded undersides adding their perfect, smooth, full-moon curves to a garden full of lax curves and rounded lines. Volcanic rusty colours predominate, with some of the open ground being covered with the local rust-red scoria.

It is not just the cultural pretensions of the arts and old squattocracy that raise a smile in William Martin's garden. Topping the columns (so to speak) beside the gates are rather surprising bristle-topped smelter-sweeps. These were bought brand new for a few dollars, when a local smelter failed to find a use for their

OPPOSITE TOP: Bronze fennel (*Foeniculum vulgare* 'Purpurasacens'), *Acanthus mollis* and agapanthus point to the sword-leaved *Furcraea longaeva*. *Wigandia caracasana* stands by. OPPOSITE BOTTOM: *Teucrium betonicum* and *T. fruticans* mark either end of a march of *Cotyledon orbiculata*. ABOVE: A sugar-gum stump (*Eucalyptus cladocalyx*), the flowers of *Sedum rubrotinctum* and *Phormium tenax*.

expensive purchase. And beside the front door, where one might expect to find a pair of ornamental urns, shiny upturned ex-army soup tureens do sentry duty.

However, if the outside world makes for some fun, the rich past of the neighbourhood is neither forgotten nor denied. An old cherry plum (*Prunus cerasifera*), very much a tree of older gardens in these parts, remains and is one of the few trees on the site. The path leading to the cottage is narrow and straight, just as front paths were in the past, and being one of the very few straight lines in the garden, makes a strong connection with the traditions of the past. To one side of the house front lies 'the squatters lawn', a well-maintained smooth patch of grass, edged with lusty bands of *Bergenia cordifolia*. This tough plant, once common in the gardens in these parts, is noted for its long flowering habit and ability to remain looking fresh and green come hail, rain, heat, wind and drought. A splendid pair of *Eryngium pandanifolium*, with distinctive burgundy-coloured seed heads, frames a view to the open plains below in the traditional manner. This well-defined, open, flat grassy space provides a mood contrast to the rest of the garden and hints at the pleasures of a privileged past.

The rest of the garden's design is as different from the cultural traditions of the past as its ornamentation is from that displayed in a suburban garden centre. There are few bed edges—plants grow directly from the rust-red scoria or from the spaces left between salvaged bluestone paving. There are few straight lines, vistas or guided walks. There are no specimen plants. Here the eye and feet wander at will, with the garden being absorbed and enjoyed from many different heights and angles. Views, visions, aspects and glimpses develop and fade as one moves through the garden and as the light streams down and through the plants from different aspects, angles and strengths. There are almost no trees or formal hedges. William Martin has rejected what he sees as a 'pampered woody European legacy', and finds many modern gardens too sheltered, shaded, controlled and enclosing for his taste. His garden is open like the pastoral country that surrounds it—free form, like the vast skies that dominate the hilltop site. The dense shrub-like *Wigandia caracasana* (from which the property takes its name), with its huge scalloped stinging leaves and large, clustered purple-blue flowers, is perhaps the most tree-like thing to greet the eye.

Few plants are cut back, and if they are it is probably for their own good. For example, the cistus which edges the front path is lightly trimmed after flowering because seeding weakens the plants. And the two upright junipers (*Juniperus* 'Spartan') that stand near the front door are also exceptions to the rule. They are clipped because

instead of forming narrow columns, they filled out and flopped about.

In this garden, plants are chosen for their ultimate shape and size and left to get on with it. They are neither tamed, trained, cut back or cosseted—which does not mean that the garden is without form, just that it is designed to celebrate plants in their natural forms and to reflect and complement (rather than control or provide an escape from) its powerful surroundings. The garden is also designed to amuse the eye from all angles and heights, in all seasons and in all the ever-changing weather patterns. William describes his approach as 'gardening with two hands—the one firm, the other flexible'.

A group of favoured plants thrive on this site, and William Martin says he has been finding new roles for these plants for some twenty years. The list includes acanthus, aeoniums, agapanthus, agaves, aloes, arthropodiums, bergenias, buddlejas, cordylines, cotyledons, echeverias, fennels, the horned poppy (*Glaucium flavum*), kniphofias, melianthus, miscanthus, nepetas, phygelius, salvias, sedums and sempervivums.

ABOVE: William Martin sits on 'Heide's Pavement', where a *Cordyline* cultivar and a *Dianthus* species grown from seed imported from the Vladivostok Botanic Gardens add pink to the palette. The grass-like *Carex buchananii* tempers the pinks with a glow of bronze.

The most important of these are the ones William Martin calls 'looseners'. These have soft foaming shapes that move in the wind and produce fine firework-like showers of glimmering, gleaming, glinting stems, seeds and flowers. When lit by the changing angles of strong light, they give the garden a distinctive character.

When planning, the 'looseners' are chosen first and then more solid static shapes are added. Sometimes the more solid plants give way entirely to more mobile, frail forms—sometimes the reverse is true. But it is the combination of the solid and the mobile that gives Wigandia its tension and excitement.

All the plants have—and must have—the capacity to stand up to the legendary cold, wet, windy winters and hot, dry, windy summers. They must also thrive under William Martin's gardening regime— no cutting back, no digging and no fertilisers. Watering is done only when the urge to drag a hose about overcomes the more attractive option of leaving it where it is. (And William claims to have successfully and totally resisted the urge to water for three consecutive summers. He regards summer as a time for assessment rather than outdoor activity.) Mulch is used only to keep weeds at bay. Evergreen plants are preferred.

Some plants have been gleaned from the old gardens of the neighbourhood—tried and true survivors all. Occasionally one proves of particular interest. A pineapple lily (*Eucomis* species) with a dull purple flush on its leaves, stems and pale translucent flowers has been sent to England and is about to find a wider audience. And an unusual (to the point of being unknown to Australian gardeners) cultivar of *Arthropodium cirrhatum*, which carries pinkish flowers, has been rescued from oblivion. Others are grown from imported seed. Agapanthus in enormous variety and in shades ranging through white, ice-blue, china-blue, sky-blue and ink and sizes ranging from thirty centimetres to a metre and a half, have been reared from English seeds. None are watered—ever—and many are producing interesting progeny. (The buddlejas and phygelius are also proving fecund in different and entertaining ways.)

Leaves, petals, berries, seed pods, seeds and stems carrying a hint of sienna-red, tawny-orange, faded-beige and deep purple—the colours of rust, fire, cooling lava and volcanic rock—are common. The odd watery semi-translucence of some succulents adds a crystal-like quality. Blues, cerise-pinks, clear yellows and acid yellows make seasonal appearances—white is hardly employed at all. The greens of foliage provide a contrast. The volcano may be have been extinct for many a millennium but the metaphor lives on, with curving, cresting waves of *Aeonium canariense* and *Cotyledon orbiculata* flowing lava-like across the crumble-top rust-coloured scoria. A gazania with a silvery leaf and a simple, small, single yellow flower ripples across the surface. This particular plant is used because unlike many of the more flamboyant modern gazanias, this one suits the mood and obligingly drops its dead flowers.

If a label were needed, the garden at Wigandia could be described as a gravel garden. But it is the plants, the ways in which they are handled, and the design that make this garden special—not the rust-red scoria. The form echoes the steep hummocky hills and the open flat plains. On nearby hills, clumps of native poa make tufting shapes—shapes which reappear in the garden. As do the dark dancing forms of the few trees on the surrounding plains. And like the trees, the garden plants move with the changing winds, glisten in the changing light and bring static mass to life. Here the sharp shades of winter and the bleached summer colours gain new exposure and an exotic piquancy. (And a sleeping volcano is always present.)

DED

RAVENSWORTH, THE HOME OF Diana and Guy Peltzer, is the sort of place where horses hang heads over fences, dogs bark and tail-wag at the same time, petals flick across grass and blackbirds noisily dunk in stone troughs. (As it happens, neither blackbirds nor cats are made welcome but, understandably, they often think the risk worth taking.) The garden itself spreads around old buildings—sheds, barns and an unpretentious house dating from 1826. It looks right—appropriate, enchanting, eternal. There are framed views and vistas but they don't terminate in mock-Georgian urns. Instead the site dictates the design, plants bring it to life and odd artefacts, garnered locally, contribute to the decoration. Sandstone was acquired when nearby Longford Cemetery was vandalised, and pieces of weathered stone are now used as paving, to edge beds, and have been turned into planters and open water containers (there is always a central stone so that drowning bees can swim out, dry off and be off).

The presentation and usage of these old buildings has changed with time. With its typically Tasmanian appearance of a neat Georgian dolls' house, the two-storey section of this house once opened its front door to the road and river. Today, draped with a wisteria branch as thick and sinewy as the body of a well-fed python, the front verandah faces a sheltered, secluded garden. The main road lies elsewhere and the river is hidden behind a dense bank of wind-breaking shrubs. The first view of the house is through farm buildings to what was probably once a modest utilitarian single-storey wing. An open sunlit garden has been made between the buildings and the problems of gardening on top of what were once cobbled yards have been conquered. Mown grass flows between beds and buildings and the lovely unusual *Iris pallida* 'Variegata'—often a slow-growing misery of a thing—finds a home that suits its requirements.

In spring, acid-green euphorbias bloom as the golden shoots of *Hosta ventricosa* 'Aureomaculata' emerge. A yellow flax (*Phormium* 'Yellow Wave') and the unusual yellow-flowering weigela (*W. middendorffiana*) stand nearby. The golden hop (*Humulus lupulus* 'Aureus') enhances a golden sunlit springtime arrangement with its sharp, acid-yellow new growth—and gets short shrift from Diana, who observes that the plant Australian gardeners lusted after for many years is a menace and tarnishes in summer.

Rosa virginiana, a choice typical of the larger plants found in this garden, grows well here. Like many of the unusual plants, it was grown from seed, suits the simple nature of the place and earns its keep in a variety of decorative ways. *Rosa virginiana*, for example, carries good summer foliage. The habit is neat and shrubby, the golden autumn foliage outstanding, the enamelled red hips decorative and the simple, single, clear-pink flowers with pronounced yellow stamens recurrent. The preference here is for single roses. Rugosa roses, with their simple flowers, thick leaves and shrubby habits, are also favoured.

The low-lying building has been given a welcoming edge of low shrubs—a lavender or box edge would have presented less of a challenge, but this mixed planting of low-growing shrubs is infinitely more exciting. Two forms of berberis have been used: a compact form of *B.* x *stenophylla* 'Corallina Compacta' with orangy foliage and *B. thunbergii* 'Atropurpurea Nana' with its red-purple foliage. The latter provides a climbing frame and makes a lovely colour companion to the dusky-red tuberous nasturtium (*Tropaeolum pentaphyllum*). The unusual prickly dianthus (*D. erinaceus*) finds a home here too and presents a perfect, if deceptive, jelly mould of foliage. The modern polyantha rose, 'Pinkie', is clipped to the required shape—and takes the indignity in its flower-strewn stride.

The more upright *Romneya coulteri* is permitted to wave a welcome by the front door, while the long-beaked stork's bill (*Erodium gruinum*) makes a home between the bricks of some low-slung steps and seeds itself with enthusiasm. (The plant, an annual, comes from the Mediterranean. It was grown from seed and is rarely seen in Australia.) Several varieties of species gladioli thrive, providing a bit of vertical thrust and more than a bit of a flowery flounce.

The garden that lies before what was once the front door has a different, more shadowy character, and bears signs of other earlier ornamental gardens. Again the layout is almost casual, and mown grass lies between large self-contained beds.

Large trees—a New Zealand beech (*Nothofagus fusca*), a pin oak (*Quercus palustris*) and an Oyster Bay pine (*Callitris rhomboidea*) dominate. Beds are richly planted with trees, shrubs, bulbs and perennials. Hellebores are a particular favourite with this gardener. Small bulbs, particularly species tulips, add splashes of clear colour. Dogwoods (*Cornus* species) with their elegant habit, decorative winter bark, spring flowers and rich autumnal colours, are used abundantly and effectively.

The choice is typical of those made in this garden, where plant delicacy is preferred to in-your-face decoration or obvious design. And prunus such as the winter flowering Fuji cherry (*P. incisa* 'Praecox') and the Higan cherry (*P. x subhirtella* 'Autumnalis'), with its long display, are used in preference to flamboyant modern cultivars. A row of old pears with wonderful shapes and delicate blossom, which once stood beyond the garden's boundaries in an orchard, has been corralled and added to the garden. Derivatives of *Clematis viticella*, with their smaller, elegant, slightly belled flowers, are preferred to the popular dinner-plate sized, flat-flowered hybrids, and are grown in profusion up trees, through shrubs and over buildings.

Colour is not eschewed, but it is used with discretion. Red berries, small patches of bright bulbs and crimson peonies highlight the beds. Orange and puce, however, are rarely chosen, but Diana observes that if bright shades are grouped together they 'get on well enough'.

ABOVE: *Wisteria sinensis* and the star-like flowers of an *Eriostemon* species mark the gateway.

Nor is eye-catching drama necessarily avoided—the huge rose 'Albertine' scrambling over and through a necessary but unloved wind-breaking boxthorn hedge is, when in flower, as dramatic as any floral display.

The garden's design is unstressed, almost unnoticeable but meticulously maintained. The impression is one of simple, suitable elegance. However, plants with strong form, shape and character, such as flaxes (*Phormium* species) and the silvery *Astelia nervosa*, are there to carry the design in winter when branches are bare and many bulbs and perennials are below ground.

Many plants are grown from seeds—Diana is an expert propagator. Some have come from friends, some from specialist suppliers. Many peonies, however, have been old family friends since their importation from Japan by a family member some hundred years ago. Others have been grown from seed. And a wondrous grey-blue lupin was garnered from the roadside some years back. It was probably once a fodder crop. Today it is treasured for its long display and elegant habit, and lupin-interlopers, with which it breeds freely, are quickly removed.

It is said (but not by its owners) that the garden at Ravensworth inspired the vogue for cottage gardens that swept Australia in the eighties. It is also said that the garden provides a healthy home to many rare plants. The latter is true, the former inaccurate, but perhaps understandable, because the garden has the sort of country enchantment that city people dream about—where it all just seems to happen.

However, it is not a cottage garden in the sense of being designed like topsy or filled with bright, jolly, common plants. The garden may look unpretentious but it is controlled and strongly designed. Plants carry the design and their pleasing harmonies and gentle contrasts combine to form a cohesive entity. The rare and the unusual grow beside the commoners with grace and good health—and their owner knows all their various strengths, weaknesses and requirements. This garden only looks unplanned because it is so well planned. And it only looks easy and informal because it is meticulously maintained by a great plantswoman.

Diana has been making and maintaining her garden for thirty-five years.

APARTMENT BUILDINGS sit directly behind the site. Houses cluster close on either side. This is inner-city Sydney, and behind a house lies a small square of precious open space. There is just enough vegetation in neighbouring gardens—a large gum, an old camellia that hangs over the fence and a massive palm—to warrant the term 'borrowed landscape'. But only just. Nevertheless, it is important. When Donna Campbell and Milton Speers acquired the property, their garden was 'decorated' with the mess of ages. What they wanted was enjoyable outdoor living space—and enjoyable did not include long hours of garden maintenance. It did, however, include dining alfresco and the peace that comes with living in pleasant, stylish surroundings. They approached Brendan Lewis, and a sun-speckled, tropical glade came into being. Today, a wooden deck stretching almost from one side boundary to the other, lies immediately in front of the house. Greenery, staghorn ferns (*Platycerium superbum*) and *Cordyline glauca* hug the edges.

PREVIOUS PAGE: A Japanese sago palm, *Cycas revoluta*, makes an intricate textural study and semi-formal sculpture.

OPPOSITE: Looking from the deck to the sun-speckled tropical glade. A golden cane palm (*Chrysalidocarpus lutescens*) and *Cordyline rubra* occupy the foreground while *Ctenanthe* species, a foxtail palm and a frangipani can be seen in the background.

The deck is kept clear of clutter apart from the dining table and a single, circular, light-reflecting 'pool in a pot'. Wooden beams which can carry any necessary shading material overhang the area, and their simple, upright supports unobtrusively frame the view down through the garden and direct the eye towards the ground and lower canopy—where Brendan has worked his deep-green magic.

A simple apron of sandstone occupies the centre of the rectangle. Deep beds lie on three sides. An edging of black mondo grass (*Ophiopogon planiscapus* 'Nigrescens') provides an unobtrusive, neat trim. It is a simple, logical, formal plan, well suited to the small area. But the formality stops there. There are no carefully sited seats, fountains or statues and no neatly paired plants. The plants provide the major decorative element, but they are balanced informally around the sandstone apron, with one leaf mass or dramatic shape being used to set off or echo another.

There are colourful flowers and fruits in this garden but they are incidental to the design. Here it is foliage that gives the place its character. The plants have been chosen for the shape and hang of their leaves and are laid densely, one on top of another. Green is the dominant colour, but it is found in a wide variety of shades and textures. Black, ruby-red, purple, gun-grey, silver-grey and yellow foliage mix with the dominant greens. Colours merge. Shapes do not. They stand out and effectively make a strong architectural barrier around the central stone square. All the plants come from semi-tropical, warm, wet climates, and all are thriving in this inner-Sydney climate.

As one looks from the deck straight down the garden, the eye is met and held, not by the focal placement of some artefact, but by an embracing swathe of evergreen ctenanthes. Here *Ctenanthe lubbersiana*, *C. oppenheimiana* and *C.* 'Silver Star' move as a single

mass and show flipping flashes of silver, purple and yellow when their paddle-shaped leaves flick in the breeze. Behind them, the large lush leaves of ginger plants (*Alpinia* species) fill out the mass and, on occasion hold the nose with their soft, warm, exotic fragrance. Above them a golden rain tree (*Koelreuteria paniculata*) links these strong forms to the gum that, happily, partially screens the light-absorbing apartment building that looms directly behind the property.

The deep beds on either side are, again, planted densely. Again shape and shades of green are everything. *Stromanthe sanguinea*, used as a low-growing ground cover, echoes the paddle-shaped leaves of the dramatic swathes of ctenanthes. Sago palms (*Cycas revoluta*) provide their perfect, dark-fringed rosettes of foliage and the occasional flash of golden-orange fruit. Elephant's ears (*Alocasia* species) flap vast, arrow-shaped leaves from long fleshy stems. And the lush, ruby-coloured leaves of *Cordyline rubra* and the grey-purple ones of *Cordyline* 'Negra' provide more strong shapes.

Above them hang more strong forms. The big green flappy leaves of a red-fruiting banana tree (*Musa velutina*) and the clear-cut shape of a frangipani stand on opposing sides. Foxtail palms (*Wodyetia bifurcata*)—a single species from Australia's Cape York, identified as recently as the 1980s and named for Wodyeti, the last male Aborigine of his clan—provide more distinctive, sharp shapes. Multi-stemmed golden cane palms (*Chrysalidocarpus lutescens*) provide the garden with an overhang of feathery fronds and will, in time, provide it with strong sculptural shapes.

This garden has a distinctly modern feeling—a feeling achieved without abandoning plants in favour of decorated hard surfaces and visual gimmickry, as so often happens in modern gardens. In fact, it is the plants that make the place.

It is also a gardener's garden. A tiny, unobtrusive garden shed and a tucked-from-sight compost bin prove the point. But it was made for and by people too busy for an endless round of clipping, raking, mowing and pruning. However, understanding the simple pleasure of being surrounded by plants, they chose a plantsperson as their designer. Moreover, they chose someone who knew how to paint with plants, how to give a small space a distinctive character and how to work with and for the owners.

The demands of this garden are, as requested, minimal. One or two tidy-ups a year and the occasional sweep are enough. The pleasure the garden gives, however, is at a maximum, and today most meals are taken outside, where at night, well-positioned lighting creates the feeling of being in a tropical glade which is lost in a world of leaves, scent, flowers and fruit.

OPPOSITE TOP: The leaf of a sago palm (*Cycas revoluta*) hovers over sun-speckled *Ctenanthe* 'Silver Star' and *C. oppenheimiana* 'Tricolour'. BOTTOM LEFT: Red bananas, *Musa velutina*. BOTTOM RIGHT: The fine fronds of golden cane palms (*Chrysalidocarpus lutescens*) hang over the glowing *Cordyline rubra*.

PEOPLE SPEAK OF BRINGING the garden into the house (or the house into the

garden), but few give real meaning to the phrase. In the garden of Philippa Macfarlane-

Hill and Alan Hill, situated close to the city centre of Adelaide, the easy phrase has real

pictorial meaning and the transition between indoors and outdoors is handled in a

seamless, seemingly effortless, manner. Ten years ago, the area behind the stone villa

that passed as a garden contained two well-grown, lightly-variegated box elders (*Acer*

negundo 'Aureo-marginatum'), a palm tree, mountains of rubbish and not much else.

The rubbish and the palm tree have gone. The box elders remain, with their stout

branches and pleasant leafy canopy providing shade during hot summer months

and framing the myriad roses and flowering perennials that bask in a spotlight of

sunshine along the back fence. The living room, from which this framed view is enjoyed,

sports curtains that echo the lemony-yellows and limey-greens of the box-elder leaves.

PREVIOUS PAGE: Roses 'Pierre de Ronsard' and 'Hero'
border the path while *Malus ioensis* 'Plena' adds to the
flowery scene. OPPOSITE: An exotic bath for birds with
roses 'Pierre de Ronsard', 'Tamora' and 'The Squire'
adorning the water. Circles within circles, texture and
transparency bring a soft peace.

Bowls of garden-picked flowers and china in similar tones stand on tables and benches. Outside the door and bordering a small terrace, box-hedged beds separate mown grass from the house. The hedges are simple and follow the line of the man-made architecture without distracting from the trees, the cool-looking grass or the dominant, deep, rose-filled, flower-encrusted bed.

Somewhat surprisingly (in a garden where the first impression is of the massed flowers lying at the back of the garden), green is the most important element and the colour used to bring everything together as a harmonious whole.

The view through the greenery to the fabulous flowers terminates in an enclosing curtain of creamy-apricot roses. Here 'Crépuscule' and 'Buff Beauty' display their lovely flowers from the middle of spring until late autumn.

Below and in front of this flowering curtain, 'The Queen Elizabeth Rose' stands tall and produces an almost constant succession of pale pink flowers. These, Philippa points out, pick well, which is more than she will say of the many David Austin roses she grows and which flower in the garden in great abundance.

However, never one to slander a rose, she quickly points to the exceptions. 'Wise Portia', for instance, which adds a focal pinky-mauve to the kaleidoscope of colours, is described by her as a 'good picking rose'. What is more (and contrary to the dire predictions found in some texts), the lovely scented, gently-arching 'Wise Portia' maintains fulsome, flowery good health in Philippa's hands. 'Prospero' and 'Windrush', which Philippa describes as 'the most beautiful roses', have been found to pick well too. Amid the wealth of roses, mention is made of the enchanting pink-mauve 'Escapade', which is described as a 'most worthwhile rose'. 'Clair Matin', with

OPPOSITE TOP, LEFT TO RIGHT: The bird bath surrounded by *Lavandula* 'Avonview'; 'Pierre de Ronsard', a vigorous modern rose named after the garden-loving court poet of France and Scotland in the 16th century; Jock amid rose and cherry petals. MIDDLE, LEFT TO RIGHT: The rare, now nameless 'Buffalo rose' which arrived on one of the first ships to reach Adelaide; A vase of garden-grown roses with pyrethrum daisies; *Rosa* 'Wise Portia'. BOTTOM, LEFT TO RIGHT: A picturesque setting beneath the boughs of *Acer negundo* 'Aureo-marginatum'; *Rosa* 'Vanity' (a modern Pemberton hybrid musk); A home for the birds between the trunks of the acers.

its exquisite, incurving, blush-pink petals, is also said 'to flower particularly well'. 'Lilian Austin', with rosy salmon-pink petals, makes 'a good border rose' and 'Dearest', a modern floribunda with rosy salmon-pink petals, is valued for its vibrant autumn colours.

The rose collection is eclectic in origin, shade and shape, and for the space employed, is amazingly comprehensive and healthy. There is even a now-nameless, rare, rich-pink, quartered, old shrub rose. It was collected south-east of Adelaide at Tailem Bend and is known to have arrived on the *Buffalo*, one of the first ships to reach Adelaide. Known locally as the Buffalo rose, it came from the garden of Philippa's late mother and holds many memories for Philippa as well as providing a puzzle and ongoing argument for rosarians.

Perennials such as the china-blue bog sage (*Salvia uliginosa*), royal blue tradescantias, cherry pie (*Heliotropium arborescens*), small blue agapanthus, tall blue bearded iris, blue campanulas, blue love-in-a-mist (*Nigella damascena* 'Miss Jekyll') and a blue clematis (*C.* 'Blue Gem') add true blues to the many pinks, purples and apricots. A rose-pink alstroemeria hybrid produces flowers for months on end, while *Lavandula* 'Avonview' adds mass and repeats its royal-purple display several times during the hot summer months. *Lychnis coronaria* 'Oculata' combines silvery foliage with white and carmine petals. Little flecks of white are added with the 'Elfin Series' of pyrethrum daisies, larger ones with *Lilium longiflorum*, and still larger ones with a fluffing 'Iceberg' rose.

Colour is laid on colour with a glorious theatrical exuberance in this garden, and it works without a hint of garishness. This is largely because the greens of the foliage—particularly that of the box elders—hold it together and frame the bejewelled brilliance of the deep flower bed and because care has been taken to keep the shady areas close to the house cool, green and open. Leafy crinums, green and white hydrangeas, white and white-and-green arum lilies (*Zantedeschia aethiopica* and *Z.* 'Green Goddess') and soft green shrubs are used under the trees to add depth, mystery and volume to the small plot. Some colour is added to these shady areas, and the rose 'Reine des Violettes' adds her deep grey-purple petals, while *Solanum rantonnetii* adds an endless summer supply of deep dark-blue flowers. The sombre mood, deep shades and shadows add a dark frame to the brilliantly lit jewel colours that lie at the far end of the garden and add to the garden's drama.

Adelaide has many pretty streets where single-storey stone villas stand side by side and roses hang over gates, but few can boast a garden as pretty, dramatic or secluded as this one. It is not large, and the view into the flowers behind the house provides the major aspect. There is, however, another delightful view—along one side of the house. Here the fragrant crabapple *Malus ioensis* 'Plena' hangs its pink springtime blossom and bright autumnal leaves while *Rosa* 'Pierre de Ronsard' and a climbing 'Sparrieshoop' threaten the fence. Destined to play a major part one day, a weeping mulberry (*Morus alba*) makes good—but slow—progress.

In this garden nature's way is the best way, and if the birds get the fruit and the dog eats the apples from 'Wandin Pride', well, the bantams and Jemima, the duck, will clean up the slugs and snails. It's that sort of place. And it feels light years away from the big city just round the corner.

LEFT: Lavender and roses. The generous *Lavandula* 'Avonview', keeps company with the equally generous Pemberton rose, *R*. 'Vanity', and a host of others.

IT IS SAID THAT 'WUNKOO', in the local Aboriginal language, means 'high and

rocky land'. And this seems likely, as the property now named 'Wunkoo' stands high

above the Brisbane River. However, there have been marked changes since the first

inhabitants roamed these hills. Today the site is surrounded by suburbia, and all visible

rock is of the cut and mortared variety. But the name remains peculiarly apt, as the house

was, unusually for Brisbane, constructed from hand-hewn sandstone with mortar made

from Brisbane River mud. Built in 1863, as the single-storey gatehouse to a grand

mansion, the house has since spread upwards and outwards. In the process, it has

achieved some status, and the original sandstone blocks have mellowed and crumbled to

the soft subtle shades that come only with weather and age. James Turner and Craig

Tanner of DIG (Directions In Gardens) were commissioned by Max and Robyn White

to reorder, restore and redesign the garden. Work was completed in 1999. The classic simplicity of the well-sited existing house has been used to dictate the style of the new-old garden and play spaces. The design is regular, formal, logical and functional. Sandstone has been used in low walls, in low perimeter-marking columns and as a paving material. White painted wooden artefacts of the garden—trellises, arches, gates and fences—echo the white woodwork of the house. The crisscross lattice on the original porch is also picked up in garden artefacts.

Raised beds held by old stone retaining walls stand on either side of the front door. A pair of tropical birches (*Betula nigra*) stands to one side, displaying rugged black bark and pyramid-shaped crowns, while clipped box fills 'lead' planters on either side of the door. The careful pairing gives a formal classic feeling to the entry area, but this is then modified with plants that take a less rigid stance and are arranged in a more casual manner. French lavender (*Lavandula dentata*)—the only lavender to grow well in the subtropics, where it is treated as a short-lived perennial—hangs feather-soft over the old stone walls. The beds are filled with white and pale pink roses—'Royal Highness', 'Margaret Merril', 'Pascali' and 'Princess de Monaco'. (DIG have found that these four modern, repeat-flowering roses do well in the subtropics.) Pruning is done in February, when the weather is stressfully hot and humid. Ever-blooming, clumping

cultivars of Egyptian star (*Pentas lanceolata*) in shades of pink, mauve and white complement the roses and 'bulk up' the beds.

Elsewhere, plants that form DIG's thrifty subtropical palette give the entire garden a sense of cohesive unity. However, these tried and true plants are often used in unusual ways or trained into unexpected patterns and shapes. For example, the star jasmine (*Trachelospermum jasminoides*), normally used as a dense wall covering, is used in one place to form a dense, bulging, hedge-like in-fill. In another it is trained to give an open, formal, crisscross espaliered effect.

The self-clinging *Ficus pumila* is used for wall-hanging jobs, and pencil pines (*Cupressus sempervirens* 'Nitschke Needle'), placed at regular intervals, add vertical thrust and rhythm. The sasanqua camellia 'Setsugekka', the scented species *Camellia lutchuensis*, *Gardenia* 'Florida' and the green-throated, white-petalled azalea

OPPOSITE TOP, LEFT TO
RIGHT: A huge pecan tree
(*Carya illinoinensis*), a relic
of the previous garden, still
dominates the space; Box
in a stone planter box.
BOTTOM, LEFT TO RIGHT:
An arrangement of terracotta
and decorative grasses. Two
different forms of mondo
grass (*Ophiopogon japonicus*)
grow in the square containers.
Zoysia tenuifolia 'No-mow'
fluffs about in the round pot;
An Indian fountain holds a
grand position in alignment
with the front door.

Rhododendron 'Feilder's White' combine their shiny evergreen leaves and scented white flowers to give decorative structure and add emphasis. A well-grown bull bay magnolia (*Magnolia grandiflora*) has replaced one lost during the renovations, and a pair of mature *Waterhousea floribunda* stand by the pool. Hedges in various sizes are concocted from orange jessamine (*Murraya paniculata*) and sweet viburnum (*Viburnum odoratissimum*). The Japanese box (*Buxus macrophylla* var. *japonica*) is also used, rather than the common English box (*B. sempervirens*). These hedging plants define garden compartments and emphasise architectural lines. Sometimes a double hedge of contrasting greenery is put in place.

In contrast to these controlled arrangements, the double white Banksia rose, pale-pink tecoma (*Podranea ricasoliana*), white *Pandorea* 'Lady Di' and *Stephanotis floribunda* add fluffier forms and foaming, flouncing flowers. An old wisteria which was cut to the ground while renovations were in progress is again draping itself along one side of the house. The sandpaper vine (*Petrea volubilis*) adds its long lasting supply of grey-mauve flowers to the wisteria's time-limited display.

The new garden is now sufficiently well grown to give more than an indication of its future character, but it is still the remnants of older plantings that give this garden its immediate splendour. Cape chestnuts (*Calodendrum capense*) link branches over the drive and a huge pecan tree (*Carya illinoinensis*) stands at one corner, making the rest of the world look and feel undersized.

The original commission specified that the site be kept level to provide play space for soccer-playing, bike-riding boys and for easy maintenance using the adult toy of a professional greenkeeper—a ride-on roller-mower. Both objectives have been achieved and the lawn looks like the work of a professional. Boys hurtle about and the grass is smooth, close-cut and unmarked.

This is typical of the way Max and Robyn approach their garden—it's there for fun and for living in. Gates link their garden to their neighbours', and the front hedge is kept at medium height so that passers-by can enjoy the garden too.

Essentially, this is a garden that belongs to a house that belongs to an energetic, live-to-the-hilt family, whose lives do not stop when darkness falls. The entire garden is beautifully lit. By day the light fittings are unobtrusive. By night there is a soft, candle-lit impression. The stonework gains a soft luminosity, water glitters, the trees throw long black shadows and the fun and enchantment go on.

WILLIAM JOYCE ARRIVED IN NSW in 1791 to serve a fourteen-year sentence. By
1794, with a conditional pardon and a land grant of 30 acres in the area now known as
Baulkham Hills, he was a farmer. And the evidence suggests that, in the area that was
to become the food bowl of the colony, he was a successful one. The 1802 muster
indicates an established married man whose servants were 'off-stores' (no longer
needing government supplies) and who had already built much of the house that has

since been described as 'the definitive Australian colonial bungalow'. And, after siding
with the government during the Castle Hill convict uprising of 1804, William Joyce was
granted a further 75 acres. However, whether Joyce Farm had an ornamental garden in
those days is debatable. Water was limited and the production of food was perhaps more
important than a pretty garden. By the 1950s, Baulkham Hills—the area that had done
so much to feed the colony—was becoming suburban, and Joyce Farm was subdivided.

Happily, Mrs Mavis Baker bought the house and orchard block and, arriving just as a bulldozer was attempting the removal of the massive verandah paving stones, secured the house and its immediate surrounds. And it was Mrs Baker who planted many of the now mature jacarandas (*J. mimosifolia*) that today give the garden much of its character. However, what lies below their branches is the combined creation of the current owner and mastermind at Joyce Farmhouse, Mrs Caroline Simpson OAM, garden designer Gay Stanton, and Colin Lennox and Tom Gillies, who lease the farmhouse and meticulously maintain and furnish the garden.

Today, a simple curving drive leads between a pair of pillars uphill towards the house and terminates in a drop-shaped turning circle. Brick-coloured gravel is used on hard surfaces and picks up the shade of the hand-made exposed bricks used in the window and door copings precisely.

Much of the garden lies on either side of the curving drive. Mown grass lies on either side and deep beds, swelling with trees, shrubs and flowering plants, separate the garden of Joyce Farmhouse from that of its suburban neighbours. The look is soft and curvaceous and throws the eye forwards to the colonial house with its emphatic straight lines, ninety-degree angles and beetle-brow roof, and to the equally soft tracery of the trees that overhang and frame the colonial farmhouse.

The plantings in the beds that edge the drive are masterly. Each colour theme merges with, matches or echoes another. An unforced balance between the different forms and shapes is achieved—as the garden matures, this can only improve. As it is, the garden comes together as a single entity. Nothing looks uneasy or forced or distracts from the house itself. In fact everything is arranged to lend this important building presence.

A Chinese elm (*Ulmus parvifolia*), planted to emphasise a curve in the drive, has its sinuous shape and mottled reddish-brown, grey and cream bark set off with the sword-like blue-green leaves of iris. When the apricot and yellow iris flower, yellow and white Iceland poppies (*Papaver nudicaule* syn. *croceum*) and gentian-blue butterfly delphiniums (*D. grandiflorum*) keep them company. Nearby, brick-coloured valerian (*Centranthus ruber*), brick-coloured yarrow (an *Achillea* cultivar) and the maroon-black flowers of *Knautia macedonica* echo the shades found in both the tree's trunk and the hard brick-coloured surfaces.

Close to the road, blue and white agapanthus stand straight beneath jacaranda trees. At ground level, their dense, mounding, green foliage adds mass to the frail tracery of leaves and flowers that hang high above them. Nearby stands a massed planting of pink, white and purple spider flowers (*Cleome spinosa* syn. *hassleriana*). Rose-pink verbenas, pale-pink tobacco flowers, rose-pink snapdragons and the strong violet shades of cherry pie (*Heliotropium arborescens*) and *Buddleja* 'Black Knight' also set off the blue-bell flowered jacarandas.

Purple ajuga (*A. reptans* 'Atropurpurea') and golden marjoram (*Origanum vulgare* 'Aureum') are used to edge the curving beds near a liquidambar (*L. styraciflua*). A pink hibiscus (*H.* 'Apple Blossom') is paired with a soft pink daylily, while erect white November lilies (*Lilium longiflorum*) stand beside the tiered layers of the white-flowered *Viburnum plicatum*.

To one side of the house the spiky cream flowers of *Sisyrinchium striatum* and pale yellow canna lilies (*Canna* x *generalis*) stand beside sandstone pillars. The mounding pale leaves of *Helichrysum petiolare* are used to change this lemon-yellow theme to mauve-purple-grey and silvery-white. Curry plant (*Helichrysum italicum*) and lamb's ears (*Stachys byzantina*) provide silvery tones while the leaves of lavenders and olives introduce a greyer note. Violet-purple iris and hebes bloom with deep plum-purple cleomes and penstemons. Wallflowers (*Erysimum linifolium* 'Bicolour'), chives (*Allium schoenoprasum*) and the highly scented old-fashioned sweet pea (*Lathyrus odoratus*) add more mauves and lavenders to the scene. The apricot-flowered angel's trumpet (*Brugmansia* 'Charles Grimaldi') stands nearby.

To the other side of the house, a venerable but graceful peppercorn tree (*Schinus molle*) overhangs a quiet courtyard. In the shade beneath its branches, white and green arum lilies (*Zantedeschia aethiopica* and *Z.* 'Green Goddess') display their lush, curved flowers in the company of the mauve metallic spikes of *Acanthus mollis*. Their elegant, mint-green, paddle-shaped leaves look well with the dark, sculptural leaves of the acanthus, too. Orange jessamine (*Murraya paniculata*) adds scent and glossy green leaves to those of the camellias that screen the fence. Against the house, in glorious isolation, stand two large containers holding an impressive pair of stately fiddleleaf figs (*Ficus lyrata*). Their curious, large, glossy, heavenward-pointing leaves and slightly tortured forms give this shady space enormous character. These plants have moved from place to place with Colin and Tom over the years, acquiring great stage presence along the way and the character of old friends who have seen it all before.

An old olive tree (*Olea europaea*) stands behind the house, surrounded by flowering plants, and screens the garden from the world outside. White mop-top hydrangeas (*H.* 'Cygnet') bloom beside richly coloured fuchsia bushes grown as standards. Nearby, a well-grown pigeon berry bush (*Duranta erecta*) showers the ground with pale mauve-blue petals. *Campanula rapunculoides* stands straight with white foxgloves (*Digitalis purpurea* var. *albiflora*). Blue veronica (*V. spicata*) sets off the ever-flowering, yellow Chinese lantern (*Abutilon* 'Sydney Belle'). Pots filled with pale grey-purple petunias or packed with lavenders are used to edge steps and the verandah, where a begonia with leaves like lilypads shelters from the sun.

Appropriate design and careful maintenance ensure that this garden has an always-been-here and always-looked-like-this atmosphere. (In point of fact, most of the smaller plants have only been in residence for the past few years.) Rich soil and adequate water have done the rest, and ensure the continued good health of a range of plants that would struggle to survive in nearby Sydney. Nothing here looks out of place, and today Joyce Farmhouse has a garden, albeit a small one, which befits its age and historic importance. And it is the sort of garden that we would all like to believe it had two hundred years ago.

BELOW, LEFT TO RIGHT: A magnificent *Jacaranda mimosifolia* in full flower and a Norfolk Island pine (*Araucaria hetrophylla*) frame the view towards the cottage; A *Hosta fortunei* cultivar, as yet unnamed—many recently acquired plants have come from other old gardens, and their names have become lost in the mires of time; Still life by the back door.

SITUATED ON Victoria's Bellarine Peninsula, where the land is open, grassy and

wind-swept, this garden was just a paddock a few years ago. A view of Port Phillip Bay

dominates the site, and beyond this stretch of sea, the lumpy bumpy You Yang hills,

with their ever-changing colours, can be seen in the distance. As one approaches Janice

Morrison's garden, through bands of young native trees, empty moat-like dams and dry

paddocks (the area is in severe drought), the last thing one expects to find is a strongly

designed garden filled with well-established, apparently thriving, exotic plants. On

either side of the house gate lie two clearly defined, matching flowerbeds which add a

suitable touch of formality to the entrance. (Elsewhere, in keeping with the soft grassy

landscape, the flowerbeds purposely merge with grass or gravel in a more imperceptible

manner.) Low-growing salvias, agapanthus and pokers (*Kniphofia* species) and ground-

hugging gazanias tough it out here during the dry summer months. In the wetter

winters a few jewel-coloured, kitten-faced pansies may be added to grace a particular occasion, but they are not what this garden is about.)

From the gate, a straight path leads through an entry courtyard to a paved terrace and the house. The courtyard's outer wall is edged with a row of pretty box-leaf azaras (*Azara microphylla*), with their fine, dark, glossy leaves, vanilla-scented flowers and red autumnal berries, and is pierced by the gate and a series of open, elongated windows. At the base of each window lies a decorative bowl of curvaceous succulents; from the outside, these are the only hint one gets of the jewelled garden that lies within the courtyard walls.

Here succulents are used to give the enclosed space a forceful individuality of great elegance and originality. On either side of the path lie two square beds. The path edge sides are edged with wide, jade-green, tight-packed, rosette ribbons of *Echeveria secunda*. An equally effective ribbon of *Echeveria secunda* var. *glauca* edges the terrace side and adds a pinkish tint to the milky jade-greens of the smaller variety. Sea-bleached shells—the gifts of grandchildren—lie on the ground like the exposed weft threads of old tapestry. On them lies a rich embroidery of succulents. *Cotyledon orbiculata* presents icy-white luminous leaves. *Graptopetalum paraguayense* adds a dull metallic grey. The glaucous *Senecio serpens* spreads an opalescent blue sea. The jelly-bean plant (*Sedum rubrotinctum* 'Aurora') displays a mass of little scarlet bead-like blobs, while the flowers of a crimson kalanchoe (*K. blossfeldiana*) add a right royal blaze. Jade plant (*Crassula portulacea*) and *Portulacaria afra* (also commonly called jade plant) sit in a blue pot beside a stone dog.

All flower well in this hot, formal setting, but flowers are not what this display is about. In fact, many of the flowers on the smaller succulents are removed as soon as they appear. Leaf colour and form are the important and effective elements here. The colours are rich and rare—muted, metallic, watery to the point of being iridescent and, in subtle watery ways, bright. Fat curves lie against square containing lines. The iron terrace furniture is painted in a subtle shade of grey-green—the shade taken from a succulent's leaf. (Janice does not like heritage colours.) Height and strong shapes are added with a single huge yucca (*Agave attenuata*) and different forms of *Aeonium arboreum*—including the mahogany-black 'Zwartkop'.

Huge clamshells catch drips under taps. They were put in place for the birds, and now birdie bath times add movement to the sheltered still life of this sculptural courtyard. And on hot days, the dogs add to this by sitting in the water-filled shells!

The garden on the seaward side of the house, immediately opposite the courtyard, is flat. Echoing the path through the courtyard,

OPPOSITE: *Echeveria setosa* grows through a weaving of bleached shells and sand grit. *Senecio serpens* can be seen to the right.

a second path links a paved terrace to a wide fan of mown grass. In design terms, the two paths—one on either side of the house—form a vista beginning at the front gate and terminating in a framed view to the distant hills. (The windows are arranged so that one looks right through the house.)

Deep, wide beds where plants lie low flank either side of the path, with *Convolvulus sabatius* providing an almost endless supply of cerulean-blue flowers. Here the species is planted with the cultivar 'Blue Lake', and the mixed intensities of these blues adds a subtle variation to these flat, flowery beds which picks up the different blues of the sea and sky. A ha-ha, its edge decorated with four stately, succulent-filled urns, separates paddocks from mown grass. These huge urns are all that interrupt the vast view but, by comparison, they look small—almost insignificant. The grass at their bases is intentionally left to form whatever tufts and clumps the wind will allow. And two larger-than-life metal ibis, placed at the foot of one urn, have a patch of unmown tufting grass to peck through. The unusual treatment, or lack of it, ties the garden firmly to its grassy setting.

To one side of the open lawn lies the swimming pool and a picking bed for roses; to the other side lie two large separate ornamental gardens. One of these, the rarely watered wind garden, is separated from grassy paddocks by a simple farm-typical wire fence. Here, wind-happy plants break the rolling grasses of the paddocks in a gentle, unstressed manner. In summer, the wind garden and adjoining paddocks share the same dry, hard look. Thirty-four olive trees form a backdrop and are enjoyed for their 'continual and wonderful movement'. *Yucca* species, pokers (*Kniphofia* species) and echiums—lots of different ones—stand in clumps and take the exposure in style. Agapanthus dominate the summer planting (again several different species are used) and are proving valuable in drought conditions. Many of the plants are unavailable in general commerce and represent a lifetime spent collecting from old gardens, Sunday markets and botanical gardens—a splendid yellow-flowered wormwood still bears the label *Artemisia* 3891. Lemon nasturtiums, lemon Californian poppies (*Eschscholzia californica*) and lemon-yellow eggs-and-bacon (*Linaria vulgaris*) form thick, flowery patches at ground level. Throughout this garden, flowers are either big, bold and bright, or form great blocks of colour—it's a place that needs and gets strong treatment. Pale pinks are rarely allowed, and even pink buds on *Oenothera speciosa* 'Alba' are viewed with disfavour.

The second garden, overlooked by the formal sitting room, is protected from the strong salt-laden winds by brushwood fences, and

cut off from the surrounding paddocks and view. The central lawn is kept green and close-mown. The atmosphere is secluded. The place is more garden-like in the conventional sense. Ferny trees with upright trunks (*Gleditsia triacanthos* 'Shademaster') are grouped on the lawn and shelter a well-used bird bath. The acid-green leaves are in sharp contrast to the dustier leaf shades of the wind garden, and set the tone for the bright clear colours that surround them.

Clear reds are used with confidence and to great effect here. Janice speaks of 'having fun with red'. Red alstroemerias, burnt-red yarrows (*Achillea* 'The Beacon') and clear red penstemons bloom for months. The New Zealand rose 'Colourbreak' adds dark scarlet blobs to the clear-red spires of *Gladiolus cardinalis*. Flooding patches of red poppies (*Papaver commutatum*) create an effect resembling an Impressionist's painting. The purple perennial statice (*Limonium perezii*) is very dominant throughout the year. A bronze-leafed flax (*Phormium tenax* 'Purpureum'), the blue-flowered *Ceanothus grisens* var. *horizontalis* 'Yankee Point', a stalwart golden euonymus and the fluffy smoke bush (*Cotinus coggygria* 'Grace') set off the reds. The frail-looking smoke bush thrives in the tough conditions, whereas the tough, lemon-yellow Californian tree lupin (*Lupinus arboreus)* has been known to break in the wind. The rose 'Windrush', bought for its promising name, also became a wind casualty.

This garden is composed of many gardens—and the word 'composed' is used here with all its implications. There is no visual jar between the different garden areas or between the garden and the surrounding landscape. Each element enhances and relates easily to the other. It is, however, an elaborately planted garden and the result of considerable plant knowledge and a lifetime of collecting. More imitated than imitative, the design takes little or nothing from any fashionable or historic school of garden design, but is the product of a clear concept, decided personal tastes, considerable hands-on experience and a god-given ability to turn vision into reality.

OPPOSITE TOP, LEFT TO RIGHT: 'Honey', by John Barter; An alert hare sits beside a clumping, spiky zebra plant (*Haworthia attenuata*). MIDDLE, LEFT TO RIGHT: A *Dudleya* species; *Echium wildpretii* with the Canary Island daisy (*Tanacetum ptarmiciflorum*). BOTTOM, LEFT TO RIGHT: A family friend; The tight-packed leaves of *Echeveria secunda*.

RAST

DUNEDIN, ANNABEL SCOTT'S garden in northern Tasmania, comes as a surprise.

The approach is along a drive bordered on both sides by massive clipped walls of

Cupressus macrocarpa. Once a year, it takes two men an entire week, working from eight

in the morning until eight at night, to clip these monumental edifices. Unadorned mown

grass borders the track. The effect is severe, oppressive, dramatic, green on green, hard-

edge art. Cars look small. People feel small. Even on a softly sunny day the shadows here

PREVIOUS PAGE: An unnamed peony seedling from the

are so strong and enveloping that photographers shake their heads. These great paired

noted collection of the late Judy Roberts. OPPOSITE, TOP: A

hedges lie on two sides of the garden, providing seclusion, shelter from wind and

massive foundry find planted with the willow *Salix caprea*

weather and a dark theatrical static backdrop to a delicate flowery, flowing garden. But

'Kilmarnock'. OPPOSITE, BOTTOM: The water garden with

it is not until one walks through a huge hedged arch that one finds the garden—and a

the strong leaf forms of *Gunnera manicata* and *Ligularia*

complete change of scene and atmosphere. When Annabel Scott began making her

dentata 'Desdemona' and a fine form of *Ixia maculata*.

garden (at about the same time as her children abandoned the sandpits and swings),

a clay-based north-facing paddock stood in front of the Victorian Gothic Revival house. The great hedges were there—and so, within the hedged paddock, were another twenty-eight massive cypresses. These were cut down, but in spite of explosive efforts, their stumps remained. This proved no great disaster. The stumps added character when incorporated into garden beds in the early days, and are lost in the wealth of plants today.

A lazy-looking, open, emerald-green lawn surrounded by well-filled beds now lies where the paddock once reigned supreme. Standing isolated, displaying great natural elegance, is the deciduous American swamp cypress (*Taxodium distichum*). Unless high rainfall and a knowledgeable gardener come together in one place, this thirsty tree, with its tender green spring foliage, rich autumn colouring and decorative cones, is rarely seen outside Australian botanic gardens.

Happily, not only does Annabel Scott live in a fairly wet climate, but she is also a very knowledgeable gardener, and the large deep beds that lie around the lawn are filled with the ordinary, the unusual, the rare and the very rare indeed. Plants are arranged with an understanding of preferred conditions and a keen eye for what they can add to the scene—either as exquisite details, as part of self-contained arrangements and colour schemes, or as integral elements in the larger architectural picture. All beds can be seen from the front of the house and all can be viewed from all sides. The potential design problem arising from this situation and from the huge variety of plant material is met by devoting at least two-thirds of the space in each bed to core arrangements of trees and shrubs.

Dogwoods *Cornus florida* and *C. mas* and the double white (*C. florida* 'pleuribracteata'), the purple-leafed crimson-flowered crabapple (*Malus x purpurea* 'Aldenhamensis'), *Magnolias* 'Star Wars', 'Ivory Chalice' and 'Yellow Fever', sasanqua camellias, *Cotoneaster* 'Rothschildianus', with its arching stems and yellow berries, the scented *Michelia doltsopa*, the better-than-everyone *Viburnum macrocephalum* and many more flourish at Dunedin.

Beneath their branches, small plants flicker as if lit by a moving shaft of sunlight. Different *Asarum* species display mottled, marbled leaves, as do elegant *Erythronium* species and a wide variety of wild cyclamen and their hybrids. Spotty dotty *Pulmonaria* species and *Ligularia kaempferi* var. *aureo maculata* mix with stripy, streaky hostas and bring the undergrowth to life. Elegantly tinted *Epimedium* leaves glow in the half-light. An unusual white-variegated form of Solomon's seal (*Polygonatum falcatum* 'Variegatum') and a rare, white-variegated acanthus add flicks of snow-white to deep, shadowy greens.

Many creative gardeners nervously avoid leaf variegations. Here such leaves are welcomed and handled with confidence and success. In sunlit spots *Helichrysum* 'Lime Glow', the variegated *Sedum* 'Frosty Morn' and the silvery *Buddleja crispa*—plants which seem to take up the sun itself—are allowed to make waves. Or small colour vignettes are arranged, such as the one made by placing a pale lavender strain of *Calochortus superbus* close to the Persian lilac (*Syringa* x *persica*) and adding the pale steely-blue flowers of *Camassia cusickii* to provide a vertical accent and slight change of colouring. And the one made by placing a pink-flowered *Pulmonaria* 'Victorian Broach' (from the USA) close to *Heuchera micrantha* var. *diversifolia* 'Purple Palace'. Heucheras with purple-bronze or ruby-bronze leaves such as 'Velvet Knight' are used plentifully, while 'Plum Pudding' more than earns its keep.

There is nothing mean about the scale at Dunedin. The paths are wide, the trees well spaced and the beds generously proportioned and set well out from the greedy hedging cypresses. Dry sunny space close to the hedging is devoted successfully to spring-flowering summer-dormant bulbs—making an asset out of a problem. The area is never watered, and in spring stout clumps of soft-blue, lemon-yellow and acid-yellow bulbs turn bare earth into a flowery fabric. (No mixed-colour packets of bulbs find homes at Dunedin. Instead, small selections are made from the best sources, the best place for their nurture in the garden chosen and time allowed for them to clump up.)

Grassed paths link the lawn and beds while the flat matt greens of the grass and hedges have a unifying, calming effect on a scene

OPPOSITE: This nameless tawny-coloured dwarf bearded iris came from a friend's garden.

which, with its great wealth of plant material and generous design, could in lesser hands become bitsy or over-busy.

The larger structural plant and ornamental arrangements also have a simplifying effect. In one corner sits a massive ferrous cauldron planted with a grafted Kilmarnock willow (*Salix caprea* 'Kilmarnock') and kept company by a rampage of tiny frilly lily of the valley (*Convallaria majalis*). Overhanging the scene and picking up the willowy theme is a corkscrew willow (*Salix babylonica* var. *pekinensis* 'Tortuosa'—grown from a twig gleaned from a friend's vase.) To one side, holding the design together and complementing the cauldron, is a huge flax (*Phormium purpureum*). The bronze-grey foliage and the great metallic smelters' pot set up a pleasing colour companionship, and their strong solid-looking shapes, the one well rounded the other sword-like, make an eye-arresting geometric study of the grander variety.

Elsewhere Pan is put in his place by a pair of flax—and rather than dancing amid tiny flowers as is often his wont, he has to fight to hold his own. Happily, his power is such that he holds the day.

To one side of the house, above a glassed-in verandah, lies a long, fairly narrow, semi-formal garden. A simple paved path runs down the centre with a small frog-laden pond taking an important and pretty position. Big-leafed gunneras (*G. manicata*) hang beside water, huge leafy rosettes of the giant lobelias (*L. tupa* and *L. aberdarica*) and the great woolly flannels of *Salvia argentea* provide architectural amusement. A bed is devoted to flouncing peonies—unnamed seedlings from the late Judy Roberts' noted collection. From the house, the view through the thick, soft, greenish flowers of *Prunus* 'Ukon' and the mad cerise-orange hanging bells of *Cantua buxifolia* 'Bicolor' is to open country. And beyond the paddocks where jonquils throng and naked ladies (*Amaryllis belladonna*) romp, the hills of the enchanted Tasmanian landscape change from blue to mauve, purple, green, black and gold. This garden always looks right, under an ever-changing theatrical spotlight.

Behind the house lie shade houses and an immaculate propagating area. Here Annabel 'makes' and trials most of her plants. She spends 'most of most days' in her garden and does ninety per cent of the work herself—the garden itself is evidence of her artistry and skill. In this garden, where plants come from all parts of the globe, the green and gold Tasmanian frog, once thought extinct, has (as inexplicably as it disappeared) reappeared. Clearly, it is a frog blessed with refined and discerning taste.

A VISIT TO THE WINE CELLAR is not necessarily vital during any garden visit.

But in this garden, the creation of George Seddon (Professor Emeritus of Environmental

Science at the University of Melbourne and an Honorary Senior Research Fellow at the

University of Western Australia) and his wife Marli, it is essential. Here, the first thing

to meet the eye is not wine but what appears to be a torrent of petrified white water. In

fact it is a cleaned reef of capstone (limestone) that lies just below, and sometimes slightly

above, the surface of this Fremantle property. It explains the faint yellow flush to be seen

on some leaves and why a friend chose to present George and Marli with a crowbar

when they acquired the derelict property in 1988. Holes must be hacked through stone

before any tree can be put in place. And this is only the beginning of the challenges that

plants face in this garden. The soil—and there is not much of that—is alkaline in the

extreme, with the Professor estimating a pH level of around 10. Moreover, major roads

lie on two sides of the property, with an intersection lying at one corner. Air pollution must be heavy. A relentless, dry, easterly wind blows in the mornings and sears the property with salt. In the afternoons a pleasant south-westerly breeze known as the 'Fremantle Doctor' blows in from the sea. (And the pollution moves back and forth between the two of them.) The rains come in winter. The summers are long, hot, dry, dusty and so predictable that if, in exceptional circumstances, a summer downpour hits the area, the semi-dormant indigenous plants suffer severe stress.

These conditions are not ordinarily regarded as favourable for the making of gardens. But this is not an ordinary garden. It is, however, a plant-happy, plant-prosperous, leafy place. What is more, most of these healthy-looking, well-grown plants are less than six years old. (It was some years after the purchase of the property before garden making could begin.)

So, how and what has been done? How have the site and climate been exploited and how has this renowned garden come into being? The answers are, as always, simple and based on common sense, and

OPPOSITE TOP, LEFT TO RIGHT: A frangipani (*Plumeria* sp.); *Stapelia grandiflora* syn. *flavirostris* looks better than it smells. OPPOSITE BELOW, LEFT TO RIGHT: Frog hollow, a natural pool; The Natal plum (*Carissa macrocarpa* syn. *grandiflora*). ABOVE, LEFT TO RIGHT: The sharp thrust of mother-in-law's tongue (*Sansevieria trifasciata*) contrasts with the softer rosettes of *Graptopetalum paraguayense* and *Aeonium arboreum*; An ornamental grass, a *Pennisetum* species, nestles into the stonework.

complicated and based on profound knowledge. Here the two elements are brought together in the company of a clear artistic intention.

At the time of acquisition, three semi-derelict, historically important buildings occupied the site. These were sensitively restored, and a fourth building, a studio, was added. Limestone surfaces were repaired and brick walls rendered in sympathetic shades. The same stone and rendered surfaces are used in the modern garden that now surrounds and links these buildings. The effect is unifying, cohesive, simple and elegant.

Walls of superb craftsmanship have been added to define important garden compartments. Some are constructed of regular rectangular limestone blocks and given a well-proportioned carved capping. One major retaining wall is constructed from uncarved rocks that have been skilfully fitted together and the outer surface smoothed to a level face—it is like looking at the gentle swirls and swells of shallow, sunlit water. Sometimes a man-made wall is added to a natural rocky outcrop but it takes an expert, or inside information, to know where one begins and the other ends.

BELOW: A young cabbage tree (*Cordyline indivisa*) sits atop a gate pillar. Alongside, a Natal plum shows flowers and fruit simultaneously.

Garden compartments, their shapes and sizes largely dictated by the existing buildings, are clearly defined. The plan is logical, sensible and simple in the classical manner. The scale is expansive and the treatment space-enhancing. The colour of foliage is regarded as more important than the colour of flowers, with dark-greens, black-greens and grey-greens predominating. There are colour themes, but these are unstressed and go unnoticed unless one looks for them. However, these subtle themes provide the unifying back-drop to the enviable plant collections and contribute to the sense of repose that pervades the garden. A wide variety of succulents are used both in pots and the ground, and the garden contains what amounts to collections of the euphorbia, kalanchoe and puya species. All are beautifully arranged and look content in their surroundings.

At its inception, the garden was to be a repository for plants indigenous to the area, and beside the front gate, cockies' tongue (*Templetonia retusa*) and the Fremantle mallee (*Eucalyptus foecunda*) thrive. However, it soon became apparent that 'maintaining a natural environment in unnatural surroundings' was very hard work. So a different approach has been explored and developed. Today, if 'nature drops in' with perhaps an uninvited oleander seedling, it may be given a chance—'If things want to grow, I let them.'

Today plants are collected from far and wide, from a palette that fits into the same ecological niche as those indigenous to this area. However, all plants—no matter what their origins—are carefully monitored for weed potential on the basis that if they grow well in these demanding conditions they may grow overly well elsewhere. (The current 'under-suspicion list' includes the ever-flowering *Dietes grandiflora* and the edible Natal plum (*Carissa macrocarpa* syn. *grandiflora*), a plant with outstanding stage presence. And the seed heads of a lovely datura (*D. wrightii*)—that, unusually for a datura, points its white trumpets skywards—are confiscated daily.)

Native Australian plants are container grown from time to time in this garden, breaking the common lore about their long-term cultivation. The one-sided bottlebrush (*Calothamnus quadrifidus*), for example, and a *Melaleuca* species which displays the bonsai-like trunk of age, grow successfully and elegantly in containers.

The tree choice is of particular interest. All are chosen for the colour of their foliage, their form, their ability to thrive in the conditions and their shade-giving capacity. (Professor Seddon believes that many trees offer better shade than that provided by gums. As the garden is used mostly in summer, shade is of paramount importance.) A large, level, open, tree-planted courtyard lies immediately beyond the front gate. Two dark-green evergreen oaks, the Californian live oak (*Quercus agrifolia*) and the cork oak (*Q. suber*)—trees the professor believes to be underrated and under-used in Australian gardens—have been given important positions. The flamboyant tree (*Delonix regia*), a native of Madagascar with a spreading crown, and the grey-leaved Norfolk Island hibiscus (*Lagunaria patersonii*) keep them company, as do the Indian coral tree (*Erythrina indica*) and the glossy, leather-leaved Irish strawberry (*Arbutus unedo*). All are making rapid progress and contribute to the dark-green, black-green and grey leaf theme that does so much to give this garden its clear character. The courtyard is brick paved in simple straight lines broken only by the trees and a delicate mosaic (the work of Professor Seddon) which acts as a 'doormat' before some well-spaced, wide stone steps. The atmosphere is mildly theatrical.

These steps lead to the studio and the wide walk that gives the garden its central spine. Brick-paved and with the magnificent stone retaining wall forming one boundary, this walk is home to a wide variety of succulents. The felted leaves of *Kalanchoe beharensis* keep company with the gleaming leaves of a jade plant (*Crassula* sp.). *Euphorbia obesa* squats like a sea urchin in a circular pot. *Aeonium arboreum* 'Zwartkop' looks blacker than ever in the heat and in the company of the silver-white leaves and bracts of gazanias, ice plant (*Cotyledon orbiculata*) and dusty miller (*Spyridium globulosum*). Contrasts in colour and form are strong, sculptural and effective. The grey-green leaves of dog's bane (*Coleus spicatus*), from Iraq and Kurdistan, form a thick, bulging carpet at ground level. Lemon-scented verbena (*Aloysia triphylla*) foams across the ground. *Hibiscus schizopetalus* hangs above. A silk tree (*Albizia julibrissin*) and *Jacaranda mimosifolia* have been established in the same hole and spread their lace-like foliage together. The walk looks cool and leafy, almost to the point of being overgrown in the northern European manner, but the area is rarely watered.

A third pivotal area lies between the house and the cottage, and here there is a change of pace. It is quiet, enclosed, shady and cool, with a Pride of Bolivia tree (*Tipuana tipu*) rising from the centre of one of the four brick-paved circles that ripple over the level ground.

At a higher level, embracing these major level hard-surface areas in an L-shape, lies a flowing area of grass, shrubs and trees. Here the rich minty-greens of pines are set off with silvery, drought-resistant border plants. Norfolk Island pines (*Araucaria heterophylla*), Rottnest Island pines (*Callitris preissii*) and plum pines (*Podocarpus elatus*) from the eastern states screen encroaching suburban buildings, mitigate the noise and dust emanating from the roads and throw the eye downwards to the brick-paved, stone-encompassed heart of the garden.

Two trees, both exotics, had survived the demanding conditions and years of neglect. A huge olive (*Olea europaea*) spreads a generous grey-green crown, and an equally splendid mulberry (*Morus alba*) survives in fine fruiting style. These two combine with the stonework to give this essentially young garden a strong sense of maturity.

Professor Seddon, who has travelled widely and at length in Europe, admits that his garden is one that responds to a mixed cultural background. Be that as it may, this garden fulfills the hopes many people have for their gardens but rarely achieve. It is tranquil, it looks right for its site, and it is hard to imagine that it has not always been there. There is a sense of security and a contained sense of place. There is spatial structure as well as a strong design at ground level. There is texture, colour, contrast, shape and form. Above all, there is a magnificent range of plants that thrive in these extreme conditions—a range that has been selected and collected by a knowledgeable, professional enthusiast whose plant palette should be on the drawing board of all Australian landscape designers.

IN THE SUBTROPICS of suburban Brisbane, a modestly proportioned front garden

has been designed in such a way as to shake off all lingering traces of cold-climate garden

design. Here the atmosphere is one of generous tropical abundance—leaf lies on leaf,

petal on petal, shape on shape, pattern on pattern, and a variety of cultural icons are laid

one beside the other. The garden is the creation of Sally and Peter Croagh and their

designer Phillip O'Malley, whose work is known for its generous use of colour,

PREVIOUS PAGE: The grass-like foliage of storm lilies

individuality and theatrical atmosphere. If there were a label one could attach to the

(*Zephyranthes candida*) alternate with stone paving blocks.

character of this garden it would be that of 'old Queensland', but distinctive personal

The scene is embellished with fallen frangipani flowers.

touches, controlled theatricality and foreign influences are also dominant, making any

OPPOSITE: Column-like spindle palms (*Hyophorbe verschaffeltii*)

such classification fairly meaningless. On the wide, grassed nature strip the treatment is

rise from a deeply coloured frill of Moses in the cradle

simple, regular—almost severe—and makes a strong contrast to the lavish decoration

(*Tradescantia spathacea* 'Hawaiian Dwarf' syn. *Rhoeo spathacea*).

that lies behind the white paling fence and the dense green hedge of *Murraya paniculata*,

whose spurts of flower lend the garden an intoxicating fragrance over many months. Here, in soldier-like rows, stand eight rare spindle palms (*Hyophorbe verschaffeltii*) which carry fragrant orange flowers. In time, their white papery trunks, marked with a brilliant verdigris as each leaf-base is exposed, will rise like columns, and their wide-spreading, narrow leaves join to make an arched ceiling like that of a Gothic cathedral. Right now, each tree rises from a royal purple-and-green spiked frill of Moses in the cradle (*Tradescantia spathacea* 'Hawaiian Dwarf' syn. *Rhoeo spathacea*) and is surrounded by a sheet of thick, clean-cut emerald grass.

Within the gate lies a jewelled, spangled, petal-bedecked garden. The original fall of the land has been maintained so that, as Phillip puts it, 'the earth could breathe naturally and harmoniously'. There is a paved front path described by Sally as having the look of a path 'that leads everywhere and nowhere—and to something'. It is bordered with low hedges. *Duranta* 'Sheena's Gold', with its acid-green leaves, is used 'to bring out the green in everything'.

Dominating the scene is a tree-like frangipani (*Plumeria rubra* var. *acutifolia*). Phillip describes it as 'holding the guardianship of the entrance garden, overseeing and connecting the house and new garden into the landscape'. The name of the cultivar (if it ever had one) is long lost, but it has been known locally, for generations, as 'Tutti Frutti'. And here 'Tutti Frutti' drops an almost overabundant supply of tinted, scented flowers onto the chessboard-like design of massed storm lilies (*Zephyranthes candida*) and square paving stones below.

A two-tiered Indian fountain stands at the centre of a raised pond and catches the quiet twirling rain of frangipani flowers—these, in the true spirit of tropical generosity, are sometimes artlessly arranged on the pond's broad rim. And behind this flower-encrusted, fragrant space lie even more flowers in planter boxes and *Mandevilla sanderi* syn. *Dipladenia sanderi* 'Merlin's Magic' throwing out sprays of rich-pink, scented flowers whenever the sun shines.

BELOW: The plaited papery bark of the spindle palm, a tree now rare to the point of extinction in its native Mascarene Islands. OPPOSITE: A Mexican statue adds to this garden's story.

A vast Madagascan poinciana tree (*Delonix regia*) hangs curtain-like behind the other side of the front path and provides a vibrant backdrop of feathery, acidic-emerald greenery. In its shade lies another richly decorated area. A flourishing flowery bank of *Salvia leucantha* 'Belthellii' stands beside the front steps, while thick swathes of green cuphea and *Ophiopogon* 'Stripey White' curve with the lean of the land. In this garden the smaller plants are massed and, as Phillip puts it, allowed 'to speak for themselves'.

Two upright Mexican canterra stone statues balance this side of the garden and direct the eye down from the all-enveloping tree to the richly encrusted scene below. And once again the ground is covered with the chessboard of stone and storm lilies. A solid corner seat is decorated with Sally's tile paintings. These have been used on hard surfaces throughout the garden and illustrate her interests in art and philosophy. One, however, is more practical and, adopting a primitive style, depicts the garden's plan.

For Phillip O'Malley, the process of pulling an old garden together and enhancing its character is more than a matter of finding plants that grow and shapes that fit. He speaks of using 'simple plans and allowing plants to speak for themselves'; of there being 'no rules in the subtropics' where 'colours don't scream and nothing worries'; of 'nature being alienated' and 'the world's energy fields being in shock'; of 'love being the difference between a pretty garden and a fantastic one' and of a need and desire 'to make space for the spirits of the earth'. For Phillip there is a *deva*, or overseeing being, for everything and such spirits must be loved, honoured, humoured and given space.

He also speaks of 'honouring what we like in nature' and, as a serious collector of frangipani, is currently trying to 'sort them out and develop better, and more unusual ones'. For him, the frangipani in this garden 'brings joy, happiness and truth', while the fountain 'gives the garden its soul' and the flowing water adds 'movement and life'.

The poinciana (*Delonix regia*) hangs a frothing lace of red flowers through spring and early summer and provides a temporary red carpet. The frangipani blooms lavishly during the hot, wet summer months and a seemingly endless supply of tinted pastel petals, looking as if they have been made from sugar icing, twirl to the ground. And every late summer downpour results in a thickly decorated, flowery carpet of upturned storm lilies. The palms add to the sweet, fruity tropical scents with the apricot-osmanthus scent of their flowers. And when there are few flowers there is the strong design, the colours in the tile paintings, the rich decorative ornamentation and the all-green tapestry of leaf on leaf to amuse the eye and please the senses. Subtle lighting at night gives an 'other-worldly experience, especially on summer evenings with the sound and movement of the water and the various fragrances mixing and wafting through the air'.

In this small front garden, foliage and flower have been combined with man-made designs to make a richly jewelled, self-contained fantasy. And the ornate character of the front garden seems all the more exotic and ornate for its contrast with both the severe palm planting of the nature strip and the calm of the tree-bordered Brisbane River, which lies immediately behind the house.

OPPOSITE: The stonework path that leads 'to everywhere and nowhere', bordered by *Duranta* 'Sheena's Gold'. BELOW: Iron, water and petals paint a picture that is both lucid and obscure, transitory and durable, monotone and colourful.

'IT STARTED AS A WHITE GARDEN, then lemon crept in—and once that had

happened there had to be blue—and that was the end.' Margaret Beard is speaking of

her progression as a creative gardener for whom colour has always played an important

role. And many Australian gardeners will find this progression familiar. Margaret began

the re-creation of this old garden in 1973. Large trees and two massive jacarandas

(*Jacaranda mimosifolia*) that, when in flower, are so striking that they can be seen when

flying overhead, were already there. A golden elm (*Ulmus procera* 'Louis van Houtte', a

non-suckering variety) that was a small tree in the early 1970s, has since grown to match

them in height, volume and stage presence. The tiled floor of a long-gone Victorian

conservatory and a superb grass tennis court, built years ago for a member of the State

Squad, were there and, in various ways, are still in use. The court is still grassed, in perfect

condition and played on regularly. Today, however, the surrounding wire netting is used

to support a flowering blanket of climbing roses, and 'Pierre de Ronsard', 'Crépuscule', 'Zéphirine Drouhin' and 'Constance Spry' hang happily in the sun. (They are not, however, permitted to take an active role in the games and face a chop if they try.)

The tiled floor of the dismantled conservatory is now the pathway in a self-contained garden for smaller rose bushes. Here 'The Prioress', 'Mary Webb', 'Ambridge Rose', 'Windrush' and Pemberton's 'Penelope' shed their luscious, pale petals onto amber and maroon squares. 'Sombreuil' covers the entry arch and frames a sundial in a pale frill of pastel petals. Essentially, this is a rosarian's garden, and Margaret Beard, an ex-board member of Adelaide's renowned International Rose Festival, knows and grows roses better than most. While she has favourite David Austin roses (notably 'Windrush', 'Belle Story', 'Wise Portia' and 'Gertrude Jekyll'), she is now concentrating on Australian heritage roses.

Colour has remained an enduring preoccupation. Peony poppies (*Papaver* 'Paeoniaeflorum' hybrids) have become great favourites, and today the deeper, richer shades are carefully kept in their colour-approved places and the deep grey-purple clumps of penstemons and poppies are used to great effect to offset the gentle shades of the many roses. The violet larkspur (*Delphinium peregrinum*), with its bluish-violet flowers and shimmering whitish stems, also makes a great shade and shape companion to the lush roses.

Some of the roses—wild ones, old ones, new-old ones and new named varieties—are colourful too, but they almost invariably display softening shades of colour gradations on their petals. Modern roses with unfading petals in solid strong colours do not find a home in this delicately painted space.

However, when and where it makes sense, bright colours are used with confidence. In the shade of a great elm, the glowing Veldt lily (*Veltheimia bracteata*) set against a clump of green arum lilies (*Zantedeschia aethiopica* 'Green Goddess'), displays its hot-pink petals and follows this bright display with pale, papery, almost luminous seedpods. A deep purple buddleja glows in a semi-shaded corner and is surrounded by deep pinks, the rich stained-glass blue of *Campanula rapunculoides* and the yellow of the elegant scented daylily, *Hemerocallis lilioasphodelus*. Flecks of white and scarlet complete a well-coloured scene which, being close to the dominating golden elm, needs these deeper glowing colours to make any impression.

OPPOSITE, TOP: White flowers to go with white flannels on the cricket pitch. Bermuda lilies, *Lilium longiflorum, Rosa* 'Iceberg' and *Helichrysum petiolare* 'Variegatum' screen the wicket. OPPOSITE, BOTTOM: An amalgam of the rose 'Rosendorf Sparrieshoop', *Campanula rapunculoides* and *Verbena bonariensis*. ABOVE: *Delphinium peregrinum* grows with the roses 'Windrush', 'Cressida' and 'Penelope', masking their nether parts with shiny, deep-green leaves and adding vertical thrust to their blowzy shapes.

White is still employed and used to great effect to offset bright colours and to add focus in mixed groups in arresting white-on-white compositions. Great stands of November lilies (*Lilium longiflorum*) glisten beneath trees and among roses and, later in the season, equally prosperous and effective groupings of tuberoses (*Polianthes tuberosa*) and gaura (*Gaura lindheimeri*) take on this important role.

Oranges and strong yellows are largely noted for their absence.

The unusual annual violet larkspur (*Delphinium peregrinum*) was found in the Barossa Valley, brought home and, in time, awarded permanent residency. (Actually, the plant grows so well in the hot, dry, South Australian climate that it might be more accurate to say that the garden has been adopted by the plant. Either way, both the shape and shade of these flowers suit the scene and the elegant, eye-catching, sculptural leaves are as decorative as any.) The liliums, a gift of the Italian gardener, Frank, have proved to be of exceptional worth and grow without fuss or bother, to heights well beyond those described in standard texts, and are now in regular demand for weddings. And the great fluffing single white rose which smothers a pergola was bought as 'Wedding Day' but, as Margaret points out, it is in fact *R*. 'Gentilliana', and has completely different hips.

Just as colour is used with an artist's touch, so shape, scale, sun and shade are handled with an appreciation for contrast, companionship, cohesion and cultural appropriateness. One enters the garden through a shaded drive overhung with trees, and is lured onwards by the flowers that bask in a bright, sunlit spot. Evergreen trees, including a Queensland lacebark (*Brachychiton discolor*), also known as the white kurrajong, a camphor laurel (*Cinnamomum camphora*), a willow myrtle (*Agonis flexuosa*) and a silky oak (*Grevillea robusta*) lie along the external boundary, giving both privacy and shade. Silver birches (*Betula pendula*) line the internal side of the drive and are used liberally in the shady, green-on-green front garden, which gives little hint of the rosy riches that lie well beyond the front gate.

Although it sounds very English (roses with delphiniums, etc.), this garden has none of an English garden's pale, polite blousiness and none of their planting clichés. Here the gardener has collected and experimented until the right plant for the place and picture has been found. And it is usually the right place, setting and companion for a rose that is sought in this country-garden-come-to-town.

And where does it go from here? Well, plant hunters never stop, but there are to be 'no more thirsty exotic plants'. Tough, fight-for-themselves plants are under examination. Phlomis, cistus and more iris are being considered. And pots of the lovely but tough *Pittosporum tobira* stand, ready and waiting, by the back door.

OPPOSITE TOP, LEFT TO RIGHT: *Lilium longiflorum* with *Rosa* 'Edelweiss'; *Iris* 'Persian Berry'; The very fragrant rose *R*. 'Alister Stella Gray', also known as the 'Golden Rambler'. OPPOSITE MIDDLE, LEFT TO RIGHT: A hybrid poppy; the seed head of *Veltheimia bracteata*; A hippeastrum hybrid. OPPOSITE BOTTOM, LEFT TO RIGHT: Ivy stems on a stone wall; A frog shelters beneath Chinese star jasmine (*Trachelospermum jasminoides*); *Rosa* 'Graham Thomas', an English David Austin rose.

'IF STUCK WITH IT, FEATURE IT', says Linda Floyd firmly, and objects that

many people would consign to the compost heap or tip become sculptures in her

hands—witty, amusing, elegant, beautiful, dying, rotting, falling-to-bits sculptures. So

do living, growing plants. Linda Floyd is an artist, and she is a plantsperson. Her

paintings have been exhibited (a process she loathes) and she has worked as a volunteer

at the Royal Botanic Gardens, Melbourne for some years—an activity she enjoys and

PREVIOUS PAGE: 'Stairway to the Stars', composed of

through which she extends her already extensive plant knowledge. At a glance, the large

Westringia fruticosa, Melaleuca hypericifolia, Eucalyptus nicholii,

two-storey 1920s house, set in one of Melbourne's more respectable suburbs and

Calytrix alpestris, Banksia ericifolia, Baeckea linifolia and

surrounded by similar solid citizens, gives little away. Nor does the garden which, from

Acacia subulata. One almost walks through the sculpture in

a distance, looks like a leftover from some indiscriminate native-plant enthusiasm of the

order to reach the front door but is totally unaware of its

1960s and 1970s. However, conventional suburban impressions soon fade, and fade

vast presence until one looks back.

completely, as one follows the narrow path that curves through a dense, bush-like

planting to an imposing front door. Far from looking weak, inappropriate or meandering (as such paths in such places often do), this one has what it takes, and gains strength from a variety of clever but unobtrusive visual markers.

For example, a march of *Diplarrhena grandiflora* marks part of the way. But here, instead of looking bush-scruffy in winter, the plants are chopped into smart, rhythmic, echidna-like mounds. (In other parts of the garden the grey-leaved *Plectranthus argentatus* is used at ground level as a marker plant, and is cut to define informal boundaries and paths.)

A magnificent clump of blood lilies (*Haemanthus coccineus*) is also used to pinpoint the path's edge, with autumn bringing an eye-arresting display of the weird scarlet shaving-brush flowers. In winter, when these plants often look no more presentable than a snail's breakfast, these ones look splendidly glamorous—like some giant gleaming posy made from plastic ribbons. (Linda loops each emerald leaf and tucks it in on itself, thus making a mess into a marvel.) Blue grass lilies (*Stypandra glauca*) are cut to make a low hedge and do not appear to resent the unusual treatment.

At ground level, the path is marked and feet kept clean with a series of unpretentious concrete paving stones. Deep leaf litter surrounds them. A branch fell a few years ago, leaving two paving stones broken beyond repair. Matching proved impossible, so stones of the same size and shape but of different colour and texture were used—wrong side up because that provided the more dramatic contrast.

The missmatch 'makes' the path—'If stuck with it, feature it'. None of these tricks are obvious (in fact they are almost unnoticeable), but they combine to pull off one immense trick—that of making a narrow, plant-embedded bush track appropriate in conventional suburban surroundings.

When negotiating a narrow path it is usual to keep one's eyes on the ground. In this garden it does not go unrewarded. Small sculptures—arrangements of natural materials—are placed at ground level in the undergrowth for the entertainment of the observant visitor and the amusement of the owner. 'A Mouse Plague', 'A Gumnut Nest' and 'A Nest for Banksia Babies' sit on the ground. Some are set off with raked sandy gravel, others lie in and on the deep leaf litter. The scent of the deep leaf litter and the cultural references made by the sculptures strike deep resonance with Australians. However, anyone unfamiliar with the Australian ethos might find some a little bewildering. Linda describes herself as being 'of my time', and many of her sculptures are triggered by news items.

As one moves along the path and passes 'The Living Curtain'—an arrangement that owes much to a rare, weeping form of *Hakea laurina*, painted twisting stems of a *Calytrix sullivanii* (syn. *C. tetragona*) and the fall of the Berlin Wall—the dense bush thins and light streams down. And it is here that the full extent of Linda Floyd's plant knowledge and enthusiasm becomes apparent.

A dry creek bed fringed with grass trees (*Xanthorrhoea resinosa*) terminates in a pond. The largest and most impressive specimen was a gift from the Floyds' sons. Others have been bought as small fellows from supermarkets (but not before the licence-to-collect had been checked). Stream lilies (*Helmholtzia glaberrima*), with their flax-like leaves, thrive here and play an important architectural role. So does the glossy evergreen foliage of the native elderberry (*Cuttsia viburnea*), with its frothing mass of fragrant white flowers. And the rare-to-the-point-of-extinction Grampians form of the tinsel lily (*Calectasia cyanea*) flourishes and flowers here too. (No-one dares move or divide it—not even the gardeners at the Botanic Gardens, to whom a segment is on offer.) Leaves from the lemon-scented myrtle (*Backhousia citriodora*) give off a sharp, clean, all-Australian smell as one moves about.

It is here, as one looks back towards the gate, that the huge scale of the bush one has walked through becomes apparent. It is also from here that the full extent, surprising nature and giant scale of the living sculptures are revealed. Luminous, long, stretch-to-the-sky trunks of fully grown lemon-scented gums (*Corymbia citriodora*), one with a sinewy rope-like coil showing through its smooth flesh-like skin, carry a sky-high canopy. All have the appearance of having had

TOP: The blue tinsel lily (*Calectasia cyanea*). ABOVE: A fine form of Geraldton wax (*Chamelaucium uncinatum*).

their trunks dropped like poles from the sky down into the soil—rather than the opposite. In sharp contrast squats the thick swollen trunk of a Queensland bottle tree (*Brachychiton rupestris*). A variety of shrubs and small trees grow beneath the trees. When three different mint bushes (*Prostanthera ovalifolia*, *P. hirtula* and *P. scutellariodes*) are in bloom, the scene below the lofty trunk sculptures is enchantingly pretty in a fluffy, frilly, English garden sort of way.

But dominating the scene at all times, and removing all hints of over-creamy charm is a huge living sculpture called 'Stairway to the Stars'. Here a variety of native shrubs have been sculpted into a massive tiered giants' staircase that appears to terminate somewhere in the star-studded skies—above and beyond human reach.

A gate set between 'The Crucified Hose' and 'A Tree Cemetery', where votive offerings to trees and compost heaps take new forms and meanings, leads to a sunny side garden. This area is different in character. A central conventional lawn is edged with beds, and for many people the dominant sculptures will be more recognisably sculptural. Betsy, a beautiful if flat-footed bull-mastiff, lives here.

The walls of the house have been painted in a variety of colours—all blue based. The colours themselves are markedly different, but they are used in similar tonal strengths. The effect is bright but harmonious. A bed filled with the dramatic black stems and dark leaves of *Alocasia esculenta* 'Fontanesiana' is set against the glowing hard-edge backdrop. One corner, overhung by a soft, ever-moving fringe of fine acacia leaves, is devoted to banks of striking silver-grey leaves. The wavy-leafed ice plant (*Cotyledon undulata*) breaks like a wave at ground level, while emu bushes (grafted forms of *Eremophila nivea*) crest the waves.

The witty plant sculptures are here for the finding, and 'A Sausagescape—Not a Landscape' made from a few threads of fishing line from which hang the living sausage-like aerial tubers of a *Cissus* species, has major visual and entertainment value. (The plant has never flowered, so cannot be properly identified.) The sculpture hangs above *Rhododendron vireya* cultivars and below the supreme elegance of the Australian frangipani, *Hymenosporum flavum*.

Linda says her work is 'environmental sculpture—and it rots'. And she lets it, never restoring or renovating, but allowing the natural processes of decay and disintegration to take place unimpeded. Nothing is thrown out before it has been examined from every angle. Sometimes a dead tree takes on new life, roots in the air and head in the sand. Or a branch is deemed better for a lick of varnish or a dab of purple paint—purple is favoured for decorating unsightly sawn-off butts where branches have been amputated. As has been said, 'If stuck with it, feature it!'

THE GARDEN at the aptly named Cloudehill sits high in Victoria's Dandenong

Ranges. With its rich soil, reliable rainfall and distinctive seasons, the area has been

popular with gardeners since the early days of settlement. When Jeremy and Valerie

Francis bought the property in 1992, with the express intention of doing some serious

gardening, the site was already endowed with a plethora of fully grown exotic trees and

large, lime-loathing shrubs—many of which were unusual to the point of rarity. In a

previous incarnation the site was the playground of a serious and knowledgeable plant

collector. However, by 1992 the site had been untended for some years, and any design

the previous garden may have possessed had disappeared into the wispy mountain mists

that often hang lace-like through the trees. Today the sloping two-hectare (five-acre)

site, with its dramatic view to the plains below, is divided in the English manner into

some twenty distinct garden rooms. All are contained, or partially so, by hedges, walls,

fences or dense banks of evergreen shrubs and trees. Entries and exits are marked with paired trees, shrubs, man-made columns or arched hedges. Linkage is by way of long, wide vistas, broad steps, clearly defined paths and woodland walks.

The scale is large and suits the huge Australian sky that envelops the site. While almost all delineation is straight and neat in the English manner, the site never loses its open mountainous majesty or the distinctive semi-wild spirit of place—much of which derives from the great stands of mountain ash (*Eucalyptus regnans*) which surround the site. With their long pole-like trunks, these trees look as if they have dropped from the heavens rather than pushed their way up from the soil and, having a claim to being the world's tallest trees, dwarf the mature exotic trees of the ornamental garden.

Across the slope Jeremy Francis has established a long, straight path that links a series of levelled garden rooms and forms the garden's most important axis. An occasional path intersects at right angles and allows a way and view to other clearly defined areas that lie at higher or lower levels. This flowing treatment eliminates any potential for confined over-cosiness and gives the garden a spacious atmosphere.

However, each garden room has its own distinctive character and colouring. At the lowest level, these formal arrangements gently merge with meadow gardens, where daffodils (*Narcissus* species) and grape hyacinths (*Muscari* species) have taken to the wild life with lusty enthusiasm. And a magnificent fully grown *Magnolia denudata* steals the show in spring.

At the outset, the strong design necessitated the complete removal of some trees and shrubs, but many valuable mature specimens were successfully moved and now play integral parts in the garden's design. Even the temperamental *Enkianthus perulatus* flourishes in a new situation and plays an important part in defining a path.

The visitor enters by way of a peaceful water garden. In design, this rectangular garden room is reminiscent of Sir Edwin Lutyens' work. The low-growing, static, paddle-shaped leaves of hostas soften the edges and by their very stillness enhance the quiet watery setting, where the only movement comes from glinting water and tall, feathery,

BELOW: *Helenium* 'Judy Sun', and *Phormium* 'Anna Red' with *Miscanthus sinensis* 'Gracillimus'. *Pennisetum alopecuroides* in foreground.

ABOVE: A parterre separates the two great borders.
OPPOSITE, TOP: The deep colour of *Phormium* 'Anna Red' makes a major statement with a sculpture by Rudi Jass.
OPPOSITE, CENTRE: The hips of *Rosa moyesii* 'Geranium'.
OPPOSITE, BOTTOM: Looking towards the water garden where a temporary display of pond sculpture is in place. Note the effective backdrop.

shimmering grasses. The odd spidery daylily and small pot-plants give a blurry focus and enhance the tranquil mood. Nothing prepares one for the visual blast of the renowned red border that lies below the water garden and in the chain of across-the-slope garden rooms.

The great red border is contained within copper beech hedges which are trimmed at Christmas time so that just when the border reaches its full flowery flourish, the hedges' new growth glows a deep, luminous, translucent, crimson-red against dark-blue summer skies. (One can almost hear Gertrude Jekyll saying, 'A flower border is seen to the best advantage when it has some solid backing such as a wall or an evergreen hedge'.)

On either side of the wide central path, great clumps of flowers put on a red, scarlet, cerise, orange, yellow, magenta and purple firework display. Scarlet wands of *Crocosmia* x *crocosmiiflora* 'Lucifer' spray out over the central path while Beth Chatto's crocosmia displays a slightly softer shade and sea-green foliage. (And closely resembles the montbretia that has taken over the local bush, with dire results.)

Great stands of the dark-leaved dahlia (*D.* 'Bishop of Llandaff'), with its great blobs of scarlet flowers, stand sentry. *Achillea* 'Coronation Gold' provides a foaming mass of golden-yellow (and is described by Jeremy as 'the best—and does not need constant dividing'). The purple *Monarda* 'Donnerwolke' and the glowing red *Potentilla* 'Hamlet' add more colour and have proved tough plants and reliable, floriferous performers—importantly, both keep to their proper places.

Dark leaves provide a night-like foil to this blazing brilliance. *Cercis canadensis* 'Forest Pansy', which is lopped annually, provides great clumps of bronze-purple heart-shaped leaves. *Heuchera* 'Plum Pudding' and the bronze-leaf form of *Lysimachia ciliata* provide more deep-dark leaves. Mass is provided by stout dense bushes of *Rosa moyesii* 'Geranium', with their rashes of single glowing flowers and red-orange flagon-shaped hips. The canna lilies, 'Tropicana', with its huge paddle-shaped, red-veined leaves, and 'Durban', with its equally large yellow-veined leaves and bright orange flowers, also provide volume of jungle-like proportions.

A massive grey-purple flax (*Phormium purpureum*) fills a corner with great solidarity and provides a sharp contrast in shape and form to the more wispy, lacy *Buddleja davidii* 'Black Knight', with its spraying luminous violet-purple flowers. (Incidentally, *Phormium* 'Dazzler', that tempting glamorous inhabitant of so many reference books, has failed to win any prizes from these knowledgeable and experienced gardeners. Similarly, many fashionable highly bred modern roses have been found to fail in this damp, sometimes dank, climate, whereas the species and their close relatives flower and

flourish here. Consequently, many of these simpler roses find long-term homes at Cloudehill.)

Dividing the great red border from the pastel border lies a small parterre where a path intersecting at right angles allows for a climb to the highest point in the garden and a view down to the emerald theatre lawn below. This purpose-designed lawn is a popular place for concerts and theatrical performances. It is also popular with the hefty-looking kookaburra that dive-bombs worms from the over-hanging branch of a copper beech (*Fagus sylvatica* var. *purpurea*).

At the higher level, this 'crossroads' is adorned with a pair of spectacular Japanese maples (*Acer palmatum*), thought to be amongst the oldest in Australia. These trees, which now show every sign of both gnarled old age and rude good health, were successfully moved and reshaped when the modern garden was designed. Today they sit above a low stone wall richly mossed with woolly thyme (*Thymus lanuginosus*) and look all the better for their new situation and for the marked contrast between their bronze-purple, deeply dissected leaves and the velvety dumpling-white cushions of thyme that surround them.

ABOVE: *Phormium* 'Sundowner'.

The two matching parterre beds, embellished with a scroll-shaped box-edged pattern, fan out and direct the eye down towards the theatre lawn. The green-edged subdivisions are filled with mounded lozenge shapes made from the dense whitish pittosporum (*P. argenteum* 'Nanum') and the glowing dark-red berberis (*B.* 'Little Favourite'). The arrangement is both original and effective, and is typical of this garden, where old ideas are often put into effect in new, different and more entertaining ways.

The pastel border lies next in this important series of garden rooms. The theme is gentle and on soft-light days the feeling is that of an English garden—on a grand scale. Shades of pink, white, pale-blue, lemon and silver dominate. Just occasionally, and to great effect, the soft colouring is brought into sharp focus with a surprising fleck of a rich stained-glass blue or the flick of a jewel-like carmine-pink. *Iris pallida* 'Variegata', the attractive oddity *Stachys byzantina* 'Cotton Boll', soft-pink bergamot (*Monarda* 'Pisces'), Russian sage (*Perovskia atriplicifolia* 'Longin'), the mounding grey-leafed *Geranium* 'Kashmir White', the lemon-yellow button-like flowers of *Santolina* 'Edward Bowles', the mauve and an unusual mauve-white form of *Salvia leucantha* all play their part. The metallic-blue sea holly (*Eryngium* 'Blue Hills') and Russian garlic (*Allium ampeloprasum*) add their fine sculptural forms, while *Salvia forsskaolii* and *Berberis thunbergii* 'Rose Glow' add more solid splotches of colour.

Grasses such as *Stipa gigantea* and several species of *Pennisetum* (plants that Jeremy uses 'with some trepidation', as they self-sow) stand high, like great showers and shafts of light, amid pale flowers and shimmering leaves. *Gaura* 'Siskiyou Pink' flutters like a cloud of butterflies, while the white bell-like flowers of *Dierama pulcherrimum* 'Album', quiver in the breeze on arching thread-like stems.

Silver pears (*Pyrus salicifolia* 'Pendula'), silvery-white clumps of *Artemisia ludoviciana* 'Valerie Finnes', fat pom-poms of double white shasta daisies (*Leucanthemum* x *superbum* 'Aglaia') and dwarf agapanthus cultivars (there are fourteen different forms in the garden) add mass and anchor the soft fly-away arrangement to its mountain home.

In the early days, inspiration came from England—notably Sissinghurst, where the dimensions of archways and plant groupings such as *Pennisetum villosum*, *Sedum* 'Autumn Joy' and *Senecio viravira* were replicated. Today the great flower borders of Cloudehill are wonderful examples of a traditional art form—a form which is rarely successful in Australia, where the climate and growth rate work against such splendiferous refinements. Whatever their inspiration and early manifestations, the borders at Cloudehill as they stand today have a peculiarly Australian persona. These borders are no pastiche of foreign art forms but have been worked out through trial, error, observation and persistence, and have gained their own particular character. The scale is large and the plantings dramatically dense. Plants seem to grow taller and faster in these borders than they do in other climates. There are no depressing holes, just lush growth and dense foliage. The flower power is fabulous and nowadays, famous. Plants are selected for local conditions rather than imitative cultural reasons. For example, the allium family (without which no modern British border is complete) is, with a few well-tried exceptions, given little encouragement here, as the majority have proved too successful for safety. New imports and newly bred plants are invariably tried but, if found wanting in any respect, can expect nothing more exciting than a quick one-way trip to the compost heap.

The majestic borders of Cloudehill are composed almost entirely of exotic plants, as is much of the garden, but the ever-present wombats that trundle about with all the sensitivity of unguided front-end loaders show no signs of complaint. The design and inspiration at Cloudehill is based on tried and true English maxims. But here, in mountainous Australian surroundings, the style has found a new interpretation and an unmistakably Australian character.

Colours look different here and they are used, with confidence, to glorious effect. And colours which in darker latitudes might appear garish take on a happy, energising vividness here that complements rather than clashes with the plumage of the brilliantly coloured lorikeets that streak through the mists at the speed of light and shriek in a happy, unrefined, all-Australian manner from sky-high treetops.

ABOVE: *Eryngium* x *oliverianum*, a hybrid between *E. alpinum* and *E. giganteum*.

AN OLD WHALER'S WEATHERBOARD COTTAGE perches high on a hill in what

is now an inner-city Sydney suburb. Three small areas—a very narrow cultivated strip

in front of the house, an equally narrow one beside it and a slightly larger terraced area

behind the house—have been given over to plants. This is the garden of Judy Cuppaidge,

a renowned plantsperson who has made several gardens in Queensland and New South

Wales over the years. Judy has collected plants of distinction throughout her life.

PREVIOUS PAGE: *Nicotiana affinis* syn. *N. alata*, an evening

Once, when she had larger gardens, Judy's plant collection included twenty different

scented tobacco cultivar. This short-lived perennial, which

sorts of frangipani (*Plumeria* species) and an entire bed of elegant canna lilies (*Canna*

thrives in cool climates, often struggles to maintain good

species). Today two frangipani stand in front of the house and attract comments from

health in the steamy subtropics. In this subtropical garden

observant neighbours who notice that the plants are better than most—the flowers are

it is grown to perfection.

larger, the scent more pervasive, flower stalks stronger and the flowering period more

extended. And a single, seldom seen, creamy-white canna lily sets off other carefully selected members of the canna tribe. Judy's plants have come from a variety of sources, in which plant nurseries do not feature highly. Often they have been obtained through the simple expedient of knocking on a door. Many have come from friends. Others have been bred by Judy herself. Occasionally, a very special plant has been imported through arduous and expensive—but legal—channels. As a result, the garden is not only stocked with some extremely rare and beautiful plants, but also contains the very best cultivars of more ordinary garden plants.

The front of the cottage, which peeps from a blanket of greenery and flowers provided by the extremely rare Malay jasmine (*Chonomopha fragrans*), is shaded by the two frangipani of local fame. And, in the shade of the verandah, hangs a splendid basket fern (*Drynaria rigidula* syn. *Polypodium rigidulum*). This elegant and intriguing plant originates in the rainforests of northern Queensland and has the obliging habit of making its own hanging basket from sterile, stalkless, papery leaves.

The narrow side garden, also thick with foliage and flowers, provides a home to one of the most splendid plants in cultivation— and one of the most unusual. This is a purple-leafed form of *Crinum angustum* that carries fragrant wine-red flowers and is known as 'Queen Emma's lily'. With its gleaming metallic-purple leaves, thick, thrusting, fleshy stems, dramatic flowers, spear-like swollen buds and considerable bulk, it gives the confined shady space its strong character. Judy found the plant (which originated in the tropical islands of the Indian Ocean) in Hawaii. She imported it and waited six years for the first fragrant flower to appear. (The story goes that this plant was transported from the tropical islands of the Indian Ocean to Hawaii centuries ago and established in the palace gardens of Queen Emma.) Today, after moving with Judy from garden to garden, it grows with vigour and flowers generously in this small city habitat.

Behind the house, stone steps lead to a small, central, stone-paved open space. Here, again, almost all space is given to the plant collections, however two seats in the sun provide a place from which this world of plants can be enjoyed.

A few 'structure plants' hold the tune in winter when much of the vegetation is cut to the ground. But in summer, the pair of kumquats (*Fortunella japonica*)—essential to Judy's jam production—play a less obvious role, and a mass of leaf and flower meets the eye. A rose-pink datura (an unusual form of *Brugmansia* x *insignis*), that points its trumpets outwards rather than downwards, stands at the back. The lovely *Hibiscus mutabilis*, collected long ago from a North Queensland roadside, stands nearby and opens white in the morning and darkens to pink later in the day. A group of canna lilies take a

TOP: A Chinese vase containing home-grown ginger (*Globba winitii*), a rare, forest-dwelling plant from Thailand. ABOVE: Queen Emma's lily (*Crinum angustum*). This rare form has wine-red flowers and purple-flushed leaves.

central position and, for those accustomed to the blatant common shades, are almost unrecognisable as canna lilies. Here summer brings the canna companionship of watermelon-pink, Thai silk pink, soft, squashed-strawberry pink and that rare creamy-white.

Unusual ginger plants add bulk and more petals. One hybrid of particular elegance was bred by Judy herself, and she describes it as displaying the best characteristics of *Hedychium coccineum* and *H. gardnerianum*—good health and big flowers with scented, translucent, glowing, apricot-coral petals. (Perhaps, in time, it will be registered as *Hedychium* 'Xavier Cuppaidge', for Judy's grandson.) Blackberry lilies (*Belamcanda chinensis*) provide vertical reed-like leaves, odd spotted flowers and blackberry-like seed pods. *Plectranthus ecklonii*, with its lavish late summer display of jacaranda-blue flowers, adds its dense form to a corner.

Flowering creepers frame the space and give it much of its lost-in-the-tropics atmosphere. Hyacinth bean or lablab (*Lablab purpureus* syn. *Dolichos lablab*) frisks across the back of the house, sprinkling it first with pink pea-like flowers and then with pink-purple bean pods. Neighbours have provided honeysuckle (*Lonicera japonica*) and the purple passionflower (*Passiflora amethystina*) that fall from side fences. Sadly, like all plants that belong elsewhere, these are sometimes given radical, out-of-season and undeserved cutbacks, or worse—indiscriminately poisoned. Happily, the well-chosen pot-grown bromeliaeds on the back wall play for the home side.

Almost all the hard surfaces are massed with container-grown plants. All have some exquisite characteristic that ensures their preservation. Spring brings the flowers of the clove-scented, yellow-flowered *Dendrobium fimbriatum* var. *oculatum*. The plant, which has acquired considerable local fame, is kept pot-bound and rewards its owner for this discomfort with an amazing display each spring. Bauhinias, *Cassia fistula* and *Clerodendrum trichotomum* (valued for its three fold display of white petals, red bracts and blue berries) live, in bonsai form, in pots. Orchids, begonias and many other personal treasures, such as the four-leaf clover (*Trifolium repens*), lead pot-bound lives—and look none the worse for it. And the autumn-flowering, sweet pea-scented *Zygopetalum mackayi* sits happily in its pot.

Judy Cuppaidge's garden is as far from low-maintenance, product-driven gardening as it could be. Her garden is the result of a lifelong labour of love, and the labour stops only when the best plants have been located, acquired, their needs understood and well catered for. The rewards are many: exquisite plants, surroundings of enchantment, intellectual interest and the companionship and admiration of gardeners and plantspeople.

OPPOSITE, TOP LEFT: The basket fern *Drynaria rigidula*. TOP RIGHT: The beautifully marked leaves of the bulbous four-leaf clover (*Trifolium repens*). BOTTOM LEFT: The Japanese clerodendron (*C. trichotomum*) which stands beside the steps is valued for its threefold display of white petals, red bracts and bright blue berries. BOTTOM RIGHT: Queen Emma's lily (*Crinum angustum*) throws a bud. The leaves lose their purple flush when grown in sunlight.

LAYE

'I LEARN ONLY TO BE CONTENTED'—so runs the English translation of the words of Japanese philosopher Mitsukumi Tokugawa (1628–1700). The phrase appears on the rim of an impressive water stone that stands with other Japanese artefacts in the North Shore Sydney garden of Prue Socha. The water stone (collected in Japan many years ago by Prue's father), along with other stone Asian artefacts collected by Prue, give a solid earthbound element to the light, leafy, silk-threaded garden. And, at the bottom of the garden, a piece of brilliant blue-green glazed Vietnamese pottery holds the eye.

When Prue took possession about six years ago, the long, narrow and sloping block was divided into four terraced spaces and an enclosing curtain of evergreen alders (*Alnus acuminata*). None of which accounted for the initial purchase. What appealed to this noted embroiderer's eye was the borrowed landscape—the leafy, well-treed gardens of her immediate neighbours and the grassy slope and mature trees of the public park that

lies beyond the garden. Prue quickly set about exploiting these assets and emphasising their relationship to her canvas.

The evergreen alders were culled. Two were left but cut back in an unobtrusive naturalistic manner, and today these two trees frame the view to the park. A small but thriving replacement stands near a precious old peppercorn tree (*Schinus molle*) that may be nearing its demise. (And should the worst happen, a future as a climbing frame for a bougainvillea is envisaged.) Prue's jacarandas (*Jacaranda mimosifolia*) link the garden to others in neighbouring gardens. A slender, graceful blueberry ash (*Elaeocarpus reticulatus*) adds to this wealth of light, ferny, mobile foliage, while a golden robinia (*Robinia pseudoacacia* 'Frisia') gilds the feather-light dance—a dance that today embraces an area far exceeding the confines of the small garden.

After the eye has been allowed to drift among the treetops, it is pulled smartly back to earth by the rich detail that lies at ground level. The original subdividing plumbago hedges (two different blues and white) have been left in place and today function as plain backdrops to the wealth of fine shades and interesting shapes that now adorn the garden. In a sun-bathed spot immediately in front of the house is an arrangement of container-grown plants. Japanese maples (*Acer palmatum* cultivars)—some of great age and all of considerable distinction—provide a fine, lace-like, bronze-purple shadecloth. Beneath lies a tapestry of leaf and flower. Begonias, with strong sun-and-shadow markings on their leaves and luminous ruby stems, emphasise the flickering sun-and-shade nature of the place. Ferns and the leaves of ranunculi add more shapes and shades, and against a fence, the Chinese fringe flower (*Loropetalum chinensis* var. *rubrum*) picks up on the dark-greens and purple-bronzes of the leaf tapestry. Small succulents add a watery, jade-like luminosity, while a sociable blue-tongue lizard adds an amazingly violent flick of turquoise-blue to the subtleties of this shade, shadow and sunlit embroidery.

Crazy paving is used to anchor the fine forms of grasses and bamboos. It also provides a place where plants with scented leaves can hunker down in the sun. Nearby stand the strong forms of sago palms (*Cycas revoluta*) and massive philodendrons (*Monstera deliciosa*), and these eliminate any potential for over-refined, sugar-sweet prettiness.

This embroiderer may play about with the merely pretty but there is also an obvious enjoyment of the huge variety found in nature's peculiarities and eccentricities: the weird and wonderful ponytail palm (*Beaucarnea recurvata*) sets the tone on one terrace. There is also a happy disregard for plant snobbery. Leyland cypresses (x *Cupressus leylandii*) and the unusual, under-used Japanese camellia, *C. lutchuensis*, with its frostbitten, winter-time display of clustered buds and scented flowers, are both used to block in the ornate tapestries. The silver-leafed Australian native *Plectranthus argentatus* is also used to provide a dense, static backdrop.

Against this contrived stillness, the yellow, white and deep purple buddleja flowers and the butterfly-like flowers of *Gaura lindheimeri* hang suspended in air and dance in unison with the ferny tree canopy of the upper storey. In this garden the total picture overrides both common prejudice and mere prettiness.

The strong colours that enliven and enrich this garden don't clash, because they come from the same tonal range. The acid-gold of the robinia leaves, the purple petals of the lasiandra (*Tibouchina urvilleana*), the terracotta-red of a crucifix orchid (*Epidendrum ibaguense*) and the rich turquoise-blue Vietnamese pot could all have come from the same handsome piece of Chinese silk.

This garden is the work of an embroiderer whose fascination with detail, arrangement of shape and form, space and volume and the tonal qualities of colour, has led to an insatiable interest in plants, their collection and arrangement. And to the creation of a garden of distinction and originality.

OPPOSITE TOP, LEFT TO RIGHT: A Japanese water stone inscribed with the words 'I learn only to be contented', is sheltered by a Japanese maple (*Acer palmatum*); The leaves of *Begonia manicata* 'Aureomaculata'. CENTRE, LEFT TO RIGHT: The purple flowers of lasiandra (*Tibouchina urvilleana*); A blue-tongue lizard proves a point. BOTTOM, LEFT TO RIGHT: *Begonia* 'Inglewood'; A glazed Thai jar with the leaves of the golden robinia (*Robinia pseudoacacia* 'Frisia');

PLANTSPEOPLE ARE USUALLY born rather than made. Gardening is different, and the urge to nurture plants or design with plants can come upon anyone at any stage in life. Happily, for the residents of an old apartment block in the racy inner suburb of Kings Cross (Sydney), both attributes have come together in the person of Glenn Callcott. And he has made them a garden. The site is challenging, to put it mildly. It lies on the concrete-covered base of a small light-well measuring about 3 x 4.5 metres and is surrounded on three and three-quarter sides by four-storey buildings. In summer (and this is a summer-rain climate) the area receives a few hours of sun at the most each day. And occasionally, a small shaft of sunshine creeps through the narrow access alley. In winter the area is totally without sunlight. This garden is on view from almost every angle and from above. The borrowed landscape or backdrop is of drainpipes, window cavities, wires and, sometimes, washing. The walls of the building have been painted

PREVIOUS PAGE: An overview is almost the only view of this garden. The palmate leaves of campelia (*Tradescantia zanonia*) highlight the design. Dragon trees (*Dracaena fragrans*) fill one corner, while a rare dwarf form of the Japanese banana (*Musa basjoo*) spreads its leaves beside the zebra plant (*Calathea zebrina*). Hoyas snake across overhead wires.

a pale, light-reflecting cream; the sky, to the viewer, is an unknown quantity—unless the viewer has a hinged neck.

The design or pattern is built with leaves. Palmate and rosette shapes—shapes that look good from above—dominate. It is only when the garden is examined at ground level, one person at a time, that the flowers are spotted—sometimes in surprising abundance. Even the rare epiphytic orchid (*Stanhopea tigrina*) displays its spikes of fragrant, waxy yellow-and-maroon flowers on an annual basis, which is more than it will do for many notable gardeners. (This absence of flowers may be due to a misunderstanding on the part of gardeners, as the flowering stem resembles an untidy protrudent basal shoot.)

All the plants are container-grown and all add shape, colour and depth to what looks from above like a flat fabric decorated with fanciful leafy shapes. The plants have been sought out one by one and stock built up plant by plant.

Sometimes one plant will lead to a family grouping of success stories. One year, for example, the wandering Jew (*Tradescantia fluminensis*) was found to look good and do well. It led to the exploration and collection of more spiderworts (*Commelinaceae* species), and today the white, palmate leaves of the rare campelia (*Tradescantia zanonia*) play an immediate eye-attracting role in the leaf design. *Tripogandra multiflora* also thrives, and displays an almost constant supply of small white flowers. (White has proved important in this seen-from-above design. It pinpoints the patterns, holds the eye and lifts all the greens.) *Dichorisandra* species and 'a few small cousins' give structure and, intermittently, flowers.

Begonias (many of them collectors' items) have proved themselves able to cope in some style, and today the impressive leaves of cane begonias—dull and dark, emerald and shiny, plain, spotted and splashed—adorn the upper canopy. Their flowers—watery, waxy, luminous, delicate and elegant—hang below. (Glenn believes that some of his no-name treasures come from China, but were collected at lower, warmer altitudes than those exploited with scientific thoroughness by the British many years ago.) *Begonia coccinea*, with its fuchsia-like flowers, blooms generously. And the unbegonia-like *Begonia luxurians* (planted 'in nodding regard to Kings Cross', says Glenn), displays great trusses of white flowers and huge palmate leaves.

Gingers have joined the garden and, surprisingly, thrive. There are three different *Costus* species, with their wonderful big, flat leaves, and, contrary to popular wisdom, they are thriving in containers. The white-flowered *Hedychium coronarium*, the red *H. greenei*, and the yellow *H. gardnerianum* all grow well. And the blue ginger *Dichorisandra thysiflora* points its amazing bluest-of-blue flowers at the sky. In point of fact, in spite of its common name, the latter is a spiderwort rather than a true ginger (*Zingiberaceae*).

Wax flowers (*Hoya* species) have been the latest to join the happy throng, and they coil along lines tied from a central pole to window-frames and from above look like flower-spotted streamers. The Indian hoya (*H. shepherdii*), the red-flowered *H. macgillivrayi*, the rare *H. obovata* and the weird and wonderful *H. pubicalyx*, with purple leaves and black flowers, are all doing well. (Glenn finds hoyas do best when pot-bound, watered regularly, given a handful of Dynamic Lifter once a year and nothing else.)

ABOVE: *Dichorisandra thysiflora* in flower in a demanding situation. OPPOSITE TOP, LEFT AND RIGHT: The exquisite flowers of cane begonia cultivars. These unnamed treasures were collected in China, but at lower, warmer altitudes than those exploited by botanists from the northern hemisphere. BOTTOM, LEFT TO RIGHT: The pendant flowers of *Globba winitii*, a plant from the understorey of the forests of South East Asia; The leaves of *Begonia* 'Silver Jewel'.

While many of Glenn's plants such as the striped-leaf *Zingiber zerumbet*, are unusual to the point of being rare, others are quite common. If a plant grows well in the conditions and adds to the pattern it may earn a place in the shade. Dragon trees (*Dracaena fragrans* 'Massangeana'), fill one corner. Kentia palms (*Howea forsteriana*) provide wavy, ferny foliage and, lurking in the undergrowth, one finds the common purple-backed leaves of a *Maranta* species.

This tiny, demanding garden has not been without its ups and downs. Builders, hail and uninvited visitors have, on occasion, wreaked havoc. Nevertheless, the unpropitious space has undoubtedly become a garden of considerable consequence. From above it looks as if a fanciful tablecloth has been spread out on the ground. At lower levels a Gauguin-like fantasy is revealed. And at ground level, smothered in leaves, the sheer wealth of the well-grown plant material astounds ardent plant enthusiasts.

MARK

FOUR THINGS HAVE MADE major contributions to the making of what is today

the five-hectare garden of Black Springs Bakery. Firstly there is the site, with its constant

supply of clean spring water, friable stony soil and its expansive view through salmon

gums (*Eucalyptus salmonophloia*) over the vineyards of the Murmungee Basin to the

distant blue hills surrounding Mt Buffalo. And there is the climate, with its cold, wet,

foggy, frosty winters, relentless, hot, dry, inland summers and fearsome winds. Then

there was the Price family, who settled there in 1871 and, using stone from neighbouring

paddocks and timeless practical designs, built four sturdy stone buildings with pitched

roofs. These buildings—a barn, bakery, stables and family two-holer (which one can

only hope proved adequate for a family with thirteen children)—have stood the tests of

time and today dictate the garden's layout and create much of its distinctive character.

The weatherboard cottage in which the family lived went off on the back of a lorry

PREVIOUS PAGE: 'Pacific Hybrid' delphiniums produce their third flush of flowers in autumn. Tiny pots are placed on sticks to avoid the proverbial 'poke in the eye with a sharp stick'. OPPOSITE: The barn, with a mature oak (*Quercus robur*), an ironbark (*Eucalyptus sideroxylon*) and an elm (*Ulmus procera*), in the evening light.

many years ago. In 1942 the Price family closed their bakery and moved away. Subsequently, their garden—and to some extent, their buildings—fell into decay. However, some of their plants have survived, and have been incorporated into the modern garden.

Their trees—an English oak (*Quercus robur*), an English elm (*Ulmus procera*) and huge ironbark (*Eucalyptus sideroxylon*)—still dwarf the stone barn and provide a dramatic backdrop to what is now the property's entry. These trees were probably planted for shelter originally, and they still serve that purpose, but from a modern designer's point of view they add scale, volume and importance to the site. Waving high on the skyline beside what was once the front path stand a pair of fan palms (*Livistona australis*) and a dense clump of variegated bamboo. (Once, these plants would have indicated that the prosperous Prices were able to add a few exotic touches to their demanding lives.)

Bulbous plants, all common survivors in the older gardens of rural eastern Australia, have multiplied with enthusiasm. Fleur-de-lis, the velvet-purple bearded iris (a strain of *Iris germanica*), bloom through the winter. Snowflakes (*Leucojum aestivum*), dead-horse lilies (*Dracunculus vulgaris*) and the enchanting greenish double daffodil 'Van Sion' greet the spring in great quantities. In autumn, pink and white naked ladies (*Amaryllis belladonna*) parade in marshalled groups along the fenceline.

Perhaps the most interesting survivor—with a history that extends far beyond Australia and the century before the latest—is the rose 'Slater's Crimson China' (also known as *Rosa sinensis semperflorens*, the 'Chinese Monthly Rose' and 'Old Crimson China'). This rose, a big bush of the never-to-be-pruned variety and small, cupped, clustered crimson flowers, arrived in Europe from the Orient in the 18th century and was crossed with the once-a-year bloomers of Europe. Thus it became the ancestor of many repeat-flowering modern roses. Then 'they'—that is, gardeners and rose breeders—lost it. In fact they lost it so completely that it was presumed extinct. 'Slater's Crimson China' was rediscovered in Bermuda in 1956 but it's interesting to reflect that throughout its so-called extinction, this rose was safe, well and flourishing at the Black Springs Bakery.

The fourth major contributor to the garden is Rob Cowell. The modern garden is his creation, and its rapid success due to his skill, knowledge, good sense and respect for the site and its past. He has given form, shape and a clear layout to what remained and added dense hedges, stone walls, an olive and lavender orchard, a picking garden, a box-edged parterre, flowery borders and a quince walk— amongst other things. A small domestic vineyard is in the making. All are progressing well and looking surprisingly mature. These additions

OPPOSITE TOP: *Eucalyptus* and *Brachychiton* species stand behind the family 'two-holer', which now makes a picturesque garden shed. The tough, quick-growing, shade-giving *Robinia pseudoacacia* stands to one side. OPPOSITE BOTTOM: Stone steps, cushion thyme (*Thymus lanuginosaus*), watering cans and an old-looking, recently planted, evergreen flowering hedge of *Luma apiculata* syn. *Myrtus luma*. BELOW: The leaves of the Boston ivy (*Parthenocissus tricuspidata*) ripple around a simple statement.

are less than three years old, but unlike many young gardens, this one does not have ratty hedges, or lines of trees in which some flourish and some do the other thing, or plants which are only 'of experimental value' at best.

Evergreen common myrtle (*Myrtus communis*) and laurestinus (*Viburnum tinus*), tube stock planted less than three years ago, already form dense wind-breaking hedges. Dividing the picking garden from the olive orchard, the laurestinus is used to form a dense and decorative double hedge with *Buddleja davidii* 'Black Knight'. The slower-growing box (*Buxus sempervirens*) is making more cautious progress, but it too is well established and growing thickly.

The trick is in choosing plants known to do well in the area and then looking after them. Rob cultivates deeply at planting time and uses straw mulches to depths of thirty centimetres and more around many of his new plants. Animal manures are placed on top of this mulch. Rabbit guards, which encircle the trunks of all the new trees, keep this rich layer of organic matter from damaging tender young bark. Water is only added when planting and, thereafter, only every three to four weeks.

Where hedges are not used to delineate the various garden compartments, dry-stone walls have been built using stone taken from the same paddocks that provided material for the earlier buildings. In consequence, few notice which are yesterday's walls and which have seen more than a hundred summers.

A central area, bounded by the bakery, barn and stable, has been grassed and now forms the heart of the new garden. It is overhung by an old peppercorn (*Schinus molle*), a chestnut (*Aesculus hippocastanum*) and four pomegranates (*Punica granatum*), each of which emerges from a dense frill of the semi-prostrate rosemary 'Blue Lagoon'. The very gnarled, woody nature of these plants adds to the area's air of antiquity. A gravelled drive, where crabapples (*Malus* 'Golden Hornet') mark the boundary, leads past the stone bakery with its glorious covering of Boston ivy (*Parthenocissus tricuspidata*), and towards the old barn. With its brilliant autumn colouring, this creeper is a local landmark. It dates from the Price era and is reputed to have come from the Botanical Gardens.

On either side of this grassy heartland lie the new garden compartments. These lead outward and upward with both wings eventually leading to the same stony hill, where the oaks of yesterday have, more recently, been joined by informal plantings of olive and Judas trees (*Cercis siliquastrum*).

To one side, stone steps thickly mossed with woolly thyme (*Thymus lanuginosus*) lead to the parterre garden. Here rectangular box-edged beds trace the simple floor plan of the once-upon-a-time

OPPOSITE, TOP LEFT: Naturalised naked ladies (*Amaryllis belladonna*) march along the front fence. TOP RIGHT: Looking out from in, with pelargoniums, French lavender (*Lavandula dentata*) and blue potato vine (*Solanum rantonnetii*). OPPOSITE, BOTTOM LEFT: Looking in from out. BOTTOM RIGHT: Sunflower seed heads. BELOW: Behind the barn with a container-grown amaryllis placed on the table.

weatherboard cottage. This charming touch honours the previous occupants and allows a stupendous view—the view once enjoyed from the cottage's front verandah.

Then at right angles, leading uphill to the vineyard, lies the quince walk. And although Rob says he likes to 'frame large views and create small vistas' this vista has already acquired considerable character and a forceful presence. Ten quinces (*Cydonia oblonga* 'Smyrna') line either side of the wide grassy path while dense outer plantings of *Rosa moyesii* enclose the area. *Rosa moyesii* is much admired by Rob for its reddish-brown stems, greyish foliage, clear-red petals, golden stamens and handsome flagon-shaped orange-yellow hips. Rob says he never wanted the 'you should have seen it last week' sort of garden. He prefers to emphasise the elegance of each season and allow such subtleties to speak for themselves. Spring, he finds 'altogether a bit too much'.

On the other side of the central lawn, a gate painted in a soft Mediterranean blue leads to a long picking garden where broad beds hold flowers and edibles on either side of a long path. Here artichokes and sunflowers rub shoulders with stately delphiniums ('Pacific Giants')—which often put on three flowery flourishes in a single season. The guinea fowl consume grasshoppers all day long—and chase away snakes—while the wild duck come in to feast on snails and slugs. (There is no spraying or laying of pellets in this garden, but the war against rabbits is both constant and deadly.)

Beyond the picking garden lies the dramatic olive and lavender orchard. Here in neat rows, well-pruned North African olives (*Olea* 'Nabtanri') sit in long strips of cultivated soil. Beneath them sit equally neat English lavender bushes. It is as if nature has invested this hill with stripes. In summer, when the lavender (*Lavandula angustifolia* 'Grosso') is in bloom, it is striped in purple. In spring the stripes are blood-red, when the wild poppies (*Papaver rhoeas*), which always flourish in recently cultivated soil, come into fulsome flower. And there are always the grey-green stripes of the olives growing from their straw-coloured mulch.

In the capable hands of Rob Cowell, the Black Springs Bakery Garden has come back to life and is fast becoming a modern, state-of-art, country garden. It is a place that celebrates its strong European antecedents, but it is also a place where the dry Australian landscape is made more than welcome. It is also a productive place, but Rob says it is not particularly labour intensive. In fact, maintenance consists of little more than mowing, mulching, cutting back and, in summer, watering—but even then only every three to four weeks.

The garden was photographed in February (late summer).

OPPOSITE: *Rosa* 'Alister Stella Grey' frames the door while container-grown *Aloe vera* plants enjoy the last beam of evening sunlight.

HISTORIC	Banongil Station—The garden of Diana and Michael Lempriere, Mortlake, Victoria.
BALANCED	The garden of Ann and Michael Duffett, Sydney, New South Wales. (Designer: Paul Bangay.)
MODERNIST	The garden of Fiona Brockhoff and David Swann, Sorrento, Victoria.
CONCENTRIC	The garden of Judy Humphreys, Launceston, Tasmania.
FRAGRANT	The garden of Meridie Hardy, Adelaide, South Australia.
TEXTURED	The garden of Diana and Nigel Morgan, Melbourne, Victoria.
IMPRESSIONIST	The Mosaic Garden—The garden of Margot Knox, Melbourne, Victoria.
COMPOSED	Roskhill—The garden of Skye and Alan McGregor, Mt Torrens, South Australia.
STATELY	Retford Park—The garden of James Fairfax Esq. AO, Bowral, New South Wales. (Current designer: David Wilkinson.)
PROSPECT	Evandale—The garden of Tim and Julie Barbour, Evandale, Tasmania.
FORGED	Wigandia—The garden of William Martin, Noorat, Victoria.
GILDED	Ravensworth—The garden of Diana and Guy Peltzer, Longford, Tasmania
ALFRESCO	The garden of Donna Campbell and Milton Speers, Sydney, New South Wales. (Designer: Brendan Lewis.)
FUSION	The garden of Philippa McFarlane-Hill and Alan Hill, Adelaide, South Australia.
LINEAR	Wunkoo—The garden of Robyn and Max White, Brisbane, Queensland. (Designers: James Turner and Craig Tanner of DIG.)
RENEWAL	Joyce Farmhouse—The garden of Mrs Caroline Simpson OAM, Sydney, New South Wales. (Designers: Gay Stanton, Colin Lennox and Tom Gillies. Maintained and planted by Colin Lennox and Tom Gillies)
ELEMENTAL	The garden of Janice Morrison, Moolap, Victoria.
CONTRAST	Dunedin—The garden of Annabel Scott, St Leonards, Tasmania.
CHISELLED	The garden of Professor George and Marli Seddon, East Freemantle, Western Australia.
TROPICAL	The garden of Sally and Peter Croagh, Brisbane, Queensland. (Designer: Phillip O'Malley.)
COHESION	The garden of Margaret and Don Beard, Adelaide, South Australia.
ILLUSION	The garden of Linda and John Floyd, Melbourne, Victoria.
CLASSICAL	Cloudehill—The garden of Jeremy and Valerie Francis, Olinda, Victoria.
ECLECTIC	The garden of Judy Cuppaidge, Sydney, New South Wales.
LAYERED	The garden of Prue Socha, Sydney, New South Wales.
CHALLENGE	The garden of Glenn Callcott, Sydney, New South Wales.
LANDMARK	Black Springs Bakery—The garden of Rob Cowell, Beechworth, Victoria.

234